BBC BEGINNERS' ENGLISH

Judy Garton-Sprenger and Simon Greenall

**STAGE TWO
STUDENT'S BOOK**

BBC English by Radio and Television
PO Box 76, Bush House
London WC2B 4PH

© 1987 BBC English by Radio and Television

First published 1987

ISBN 0 946675 26 0

Printed in Great Britain by Jolly and Barber, Rugby

The authors would like to thank all those who have helped and encouraged us during the preparation of *BBC Beginners' English*. Particular thanks go to the following:

Editorial coordination Lucy McCullagh, Ken Singleton
Design Ian Wileman
Cover design Jim Wire
Cover photograph Jerry Young
Commissioned photography Peter Lake
Picture research Liz Rudoff, Jan Dalley
Illustrations Judy Brown, Mohsen, Peter Bailey, Tracey Chapman, Peter McClure, Neil Meacher, Colin Mier, Shona Cameron, Simon Stern, Alan Rowe, Glynn Wyles

We would also like to thank Mike Garton-Sprenger for sharing his views; Nigel Acheson as the BBC producer who went to Sri Lanka; and Arthur C. Clarke for allowing us to use his material.

Acknowledgements
We are grateful to the following for their help in location photography: The Abbotsford, Edinburgh; Eastern Scottish Omnibuses, Edinburgh; Historic Buildings and Monuments, Edinburgh; Holiday Inn, Slough; King's Theatre, Edinburgh; Martinez Spanish Restaurant, London; National Gallery of Scotland, Edinburgh; Royal Museum of Scotland, Edinburgh; Wingspan Travel Agents Ltd, London.

We would like to thank the following for permission to reproduce photographs: AA Photo Library, pp. 70–71; Nigel Acheson, pp. 96, 97; BBC Hulton Picture Library, p. 95; Janet and Colin Bord, p. 98; British Airways, p.79; Britain on View (BTA/ETB), pp. 33, 38–9; J. Allan Cash Photolibrary, pp. 59, 69, 86; Compix, pp. 7, 84; Daily Telegraph Colour Library, p. 86; Featurepix Colour Library, pp. 58, 65; Joel Finler Collection, p.114; Fortean Picture Library, p. 73; Simon Greenall, p. 94; Sally and Richard Greenhill, p.27; Heathrow Airport Ltd, p. 116; Kobal Collection, pp. 90, 91; Collection State Museum Kröller-Müller, Otterlo, The Netherlands: Paul Signac, *Breakfast*, p. 83; Mars Confectionery, p. 26; Lee Miller Archives: Pablo Picasso, *Woman Weeping* (1937) © DACS 1987, Joan Miró, *Tête de Paysan Catalan* (1925) © ADAGP 1987, p.64; Oficina Olimpica, Barcelona, p.123; Patronat Municipal de Turisme de Barcelona, pp. 30, 64; Popperfoto, p.103; Rex Features, p. 106; Scottish Tourist Board, pp. 33, 34, 35, 60; Ken Singleton, pp. 79, 92, 93; Spectrum Colour Library, p. 30; Frank Spooner Pictures, pp. 77, 112, 113, 115; Tony Stone Associates, pp. 7, 21, 62, 75, 104; Tate Gallery, London, p.83; Wayland Publishers Ltd, p. 76; Zefa Picture Library, pp. 56, 59, 68, 105.

We would like to thank the following for permission to reproduce extracts: Aitken and Stone Ltd for an extract from *The Kingdom by the Sea* by Paul Theroux, p. 75; Ceylon Tea Bureau for information, p. 56; Collins Publishers for stories adapted from *Mysterious World* by Arthur C. Clarke, p. 99; Fontana Books for test adapted from *The Book of Tests* by Michael Nathenson, pp. 52–3; Harrap Ltd for text adapted from *This Haunted Isle* by Peter Underwood, p. 60; Her Majesty's Stationery Office for material from *On the Road in Great Britain*, reproduced with the permission of the Controller, p. 70; David Higham Associates Ltd for extracts from an interview with Arthur C. Clarke and from the book *2001: A Space Odyssey*, pp. 112–15; Octopus Books Ltd for story adapted from *The World's Greatest Mistakes* by Nigel Blundell, p. 46; Radio 4 for extracts from *Bookshelf Special* (audiocassettes); Sealink Ferries' *Connections* magazine for magic trick, p. 82; Wayland (Publishers) Ltd, Hove for text adapted from *We Live in Spain* by Richard Bristow, p. 76.

Contents

4

Introduction

In this book you are going to meet:

Hello!

Robert MacDonald

Jean O'Hara

How do you do?

Hello!

David Piper

You are going to visit:

Sri Lanka, a tropical island where English is a second language.

Barcelona in Spain, visited by thousands of English-speaking tourists every year.

Edinburgh, the capital of Scotland.

Talking about people

1 Work in pairs. This is a picture of Jean O'Hara, who is a representative for a travel company in Barcelona. Where do you think she's from? Where is she at the moment? What do you think she's doing?

2  Listen for specific information. First copy the chart. Then listen to the conversation and fill in Jean O'Hara's details.

NAME:
Jean O'Hara
NATIONALITY:
ACCOMMODATION:
OCCUPATION:
PLACE OF WORK:

Work in pairs and check your answers.

3 Match the questions with the appropriate responses.

1 Sorry – what's your name again?
2 How do you do?
3 Where are you from?
4 Where do you live?
5 What do you do?
6 Where do you work?
7 Have you been to London before?

A I'm an engineer.
B No, this is my first visit.
C Antonio Gotti.
D How do you do?
E At the Fiat factory in Turin.
F I'm from Italy.
G In a flat in Turin.

Work in pairs and check your answers.

4 Work in pairs. Find out about each other and make a chart like the one in 2 with your partner's details.

5 Work in pairs. Read for specific information. Make a chart like the one in 2.

STUDENT **A**

Complete your chart with details about Robert MacDonald.

Robert MacDonald's parents are from Scotland, but he's Canadian. He lives in an apartment in the centre of Toronto. He's a salesman and he works for a company in Toronto which produces computer games.

Now ask Student B questions about David Piper, and make a chart with his details.

STUDENT **B**

Complete your chart with details about David Piper.

David Piper is English, and he lives with his wife and two children in a house in West London. He's a radio producer and he works for the BBC at Broadcasting House in Central London.

Now ask Student A questions about Robert MacDonald, and make a chart with his details.

Where's (*name*) from?	He's from . . .
Where does he live?	He lives in . . .

What does he do?	He's a/an . . .
Where does he work?	He works . . .

6 Tell other students about yourself and your partner. Find out about two other students and make charts with their details.

7 Write a profile of one of the students in your class. Use the passages in 5 to help you.

Say:
- where he's/she's from
- where he/she lives or is staying
- what he/she does
- where he/she works

8 Build your vocabulary. Work in pairs. Look at these words to describe character. Which words do you know?

shy	anxious	sensitive
bad-tempered	serious	kind
charming	proud	hard-working
lazy	friendly	selfish
calm	reliable	patient

Ask your partner about words you don't understand.

Example: – What does 'anxious' mean?
            – It means that you often worry
                about things.

What does . . . mean?	It means that you	never . . . sometimes . . . often . . . usually . . . always . . .

9 Work in pairs. Look at the photographs of David, Jean and Robert. What do you think they are like? Which of the adjectives in 8 might describe their characters?

He/She looks I think he's/she's	very . . . quite/rather . . . a little . . .
He/She doesn't look I don't think he's/she's	(at all) . . .

10 🔲 Listen to David's boss talking about him. Look at the adjectives in 8 and note the ones you hear.

11 Match the adjectives you heard in 10 with the phrases below which explain them.

Example: a bad-tempered person → someone who often gets angry

someone who | doesn't panic
usually works very hard
often gets angry
doesn't often laugh
is always pleasant to other people

12 Read and predict. This is a character reference for Jean's new employer, but some of the words are missing. Fill in the blanks with suitable adjectives from the list in 8.

Check your answers with another student.
Then write a short character reference for David.

Jean has worked for our organisation as a tour guide for six months. She is c.... and f.... and has always been popular with both the tourists and her colleagues. She is very r.... and she never forgets anything. She is always p.... with difficult customers and she doesn't show that she's a.... when things go wrong. She is sometimes a little s.... if people make complaints, but she is an excellent guide whom we are very sorry to lose.

13 🔲 Listen for main ideas. Here is Robert's mother talking about her son. What is he like? Which adjectives can you use to describe his character?

14 How do you feel about:

- meeting people?
- noisy children?
- making mistakes?
- losing things?

- people who are always late?
- cats?
- doing nothing?
- working hard?

| I like
I don't like
I don't mind | . . .
—ing . . . |

Find someone in your class who likes and dislikes the same things as you. Do you think your characters are similar?

15 Work in pairs. Think of a famous person. Make a list of adjectives which describe him/her. Try to think of examples to explain your choice of adjectives.

Example: He isn't at all shy – he likes meeting people.

Now write a description of the famous person's character.
Describe his/her personal qualities: He's charming but he's rather proud. (*Give examples*)
        feelings: She likes meeting people.
        professional qualities: He's hardworking and reliable. (*Give examples*)

Pronunciation and Structure Review: page 128.

2 Talking about work

1 Read and predict. Work in pairs. Look at this magazine article about David Piper and guess what the missing words are.

PEOPLE AT WORK
David Piper – Radio Producer

I ... for BBC Radio 4 in London as a producer in a features department. I sometimes ... abroad to make programmes – three or four times a year. I ... work at 9.30 a.m. and I ... at 5.30 p.m. On a typical day, I ... a lot of phone calls, trying to contact people and organise interviews. I ... programmes in the studio about twice a week. And of course, I ... a lot of time editing. You often ... several hours of tape for a thirty-minute programme, so you ... cut the material to fit the time. We ... a meeting every week to discuss regular programmes, and the whole department ... once a fortnight. Every two or three months, there ... a meeting with the Controller of Radio 4 to discuss new ideas for programmes.

I ... angry when someone ... to turn up for an interview, but most of the time I ... my work enormously. I particularly ... radio because it ... so simple – you only ... a tape recorder and a voice to make a radio programme.

2 Here is a list of the missing words. Fill in the blanks with the verbs in the correct form of the present simple tense.

be (× 2)	enjoy	finish	forget
get	have	have to	like
make	meet	need	record (× 2)
spend	start	travel	work

3   Predict before listening. A journalist interviewed David Piper for the magazine article. Look at these questions. Which ones do you think the journalist asked?

How old are you?
What do you have to do in your job?
Where do you work?
Do you travel a lot?
Are you married?
Is there anything that you don't like about your work?

Where do you live?
What do you like doing in your free time?
How often do you go to meetings?
How many countries have you visited?
Do you like your job?
What do you mean by 'editing'?

4    Listen for specific information. Listen and check your answers to 3. Some of the information you hear is different from the information you read in 1. Answer the questions by writing down what David actually says.

1   How often does he travel abroad?
2   How often does he record programmes in the studio?
3   How often does he meet to discuss regular programmes?
4   How often does the whole department meet?
5   How often are there meetings with the Controller of Radio 4?

How often . . . ?	Once/Twice/Three times a week/month/year. Every day/week/month. Every two weeks/six months.

5   Work in pairs. Act out the conversation between David Piper and the interviewer.

6   Choose five questions from the list in 3, and find out about other students' jobs/ideal jobs. Talk about your job/ideal job.

7   Write a short description of your partner's job/ideal job. Use the passage in 1 to help you.

Say:
- what he/she does and where he/she works
- when he/she starts/finishes work
- what he/she has to do
- what he/she likes about the job
- what he/she doesn't like about the job

13

8 Look at the pictures. Match them with the jobs below.

doctor   builder   pilot   waitress

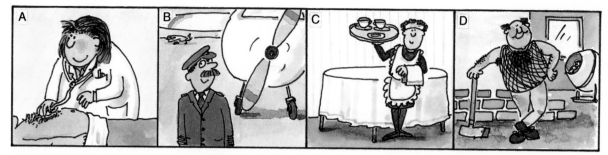

9 Build your vocabulary. Work in pairs. For each job in 8, choose the three most important adjectives to describe what you need to be.

To be a/an . . . you	must have to need to	be	strong polite accurate confident calm	hard-working quick-thinking friendly sensible reliable	patient careful efficient kind charming

10 📼 **Listen for main ideas. You are going to hear two people talking about their work. Decide which of the jobs in 8 they are talking about.**

11 📼 **Listen again. Which adjectives in 9 did you hear? Write them down.**

12 Work in pairs. Say what qualities you need for the other two jobs.

13 What qualities do you need for the following jobs?

zoo keeper   lorry driver   salesman/saleswoman   architect
nurse   travel agent   travel representative   mechanic

14 Work in pairs. Say what skills you need for the jobs in 8 and 13. Choose from this list:

You must You have to You need to	be able to know how to	drive. work in a team. concentrate for long periods. deal with problems. look after people. speak a foreign language.
	be good at	making business deals. talking on the phone. looking after animals. designing things. using tools.

Example: To be a doctor, you must be able to look after people.

15 Choose two jobs and write a short description of the qualities and skills needed.

Example: To be a nurse, you need to be kind and you have to know how to look after people. You
must be good at keeping calm and you have to work very hard.

16   Work in pairs. You are planning an expedition to get from Y to Z on the map with your partner and three other people. These people all want to join the expedition:

Jones, a doctor   Blake, a mechanic
Smith, an athlete   Crane, a cook
Ryan, an explorer   Mills, a hunter

STUDENT **A**

You know some facts about the people which Student **B** doesn't know.

Dr Jones knows how to shoot.
Crane can't swim.
Ryan is afraid of heights.
Mills is good at climbing.
Smith doesn't know how to work in a team.
Blake was born in the jungle.

STUDENT **B**

You know some facts about the people which Student **A** doesn't know.

Dr Jones is nearly sixty.
Smith knows how to fly a helicopter.
Blake was once in prison for armed robbery.
Crane was a soldier.
Ryan is good at building boats.
Mills can't swim.

Look carefully at the map, and discuss which three people make the best team to go on the expedition. Write a paragraph giving your reasons.

Pronunciation and Structure Review: page 130.

3 Describing appearance

1 Read for specific information. Robert MacDonald and his cousin Annie have not seen each other for fifteen years. Read Annie's letter to Robert.

Find out:
- how old she is
- how tall she is
- what build she is
- what colour eyes she's got
- what her hair's like
- if she's got any special features

take some time off work, I'll be at Waverley Station to meet you. But I don't know if you'll recognise me any more – after all, I was only five years old when you went to Canada! I haven't got a photo to send you so I ought to tell you what I look like. I'm tall, about 5'9", and I've got blue eyes. As for my hair – well, I had shoulder-length straight dark hair until a month ago, but now it's curly and auburn – I'm not sure if I like it yet! I'm slim – well, quite slim, but I'd like to lose a few pounds... I usually wear jeans and a T-shirt, but if I come from work, I'll be in a skirt and blouse. I've got a photo of you taken when you were twelve, but I expect you've changed. What do you look like now?

2 Build your vocabulary. Put these words under the correct headings:

AGE   HEIGHT   BUILD   EYES
HAIR   SPECIAL FEATURES

young	long	dark
slim	short	brown
red	curly	tall
fat	straight	bald
auburn	grey	beard
average	blonde	old
glasses	black	moustache
middle-aged	thin	blue

Which of these words can go under two headings?

3 Work in pairs. Look at Annie's photo of Robert. What does he look like in the photo?

What does he look like?	He's (*age/height/build*) with ... (*hair/eyes*). He's got (*hair/eyes/special features*).

4 Work in pairs. Look at the photo of Robert on page 6. Say how he has changed.

Example: He had longer hair when he was twelve. Now it's shorter.

5 Annie's photo of Robert is thirteen years old. Write sentences describing what Robert looks like now in the photo on page 6.

Describe:
- how old he is
- how tall he is
- what build he is
- what colour eyes he's got
- what his hair's like
- any special features

6 Have you changed since you were younger? Tell another student what you looked like.

Example: — I had long hair when I was young.
— Did you? I was much slimmer.

7 Work in pairs. The people in the photograph are all waiting at Waverley Station when Robert arrives. Which one is Annie?

Example: — I think this is Annie. She's quite tall.
— No, her hair's <u>too</u> short. It <u>isn't</u> long <u>enough</u>.

8 📼 Listen for main ideas. Listen to three people in the picture describing themselves. Decide who is speaking in each case.

9 Read and predict. Try to fill in the blanks in the dialogue.

WOMAN:	Darling! It's wonderful to see you after so long. How . . . ?
ROBERT:	Hello, are you Annie MacDonald?
WOMAN:	No, . . . ! Are you Harry Goldblum?
ROBERT:	No, . . . !
WOMAN:	That's amazing! You look . . . .
ROBERT:	I'm sorry. I'm . . . Annie MacDonald. Have you seen her? She's tall, with . . . . Annie! How . . . ? It's . . . to see you again.
WOMAN:	That's all very well for you, but where's Harry?

📼 Listen for specific information. Listen and check.

10 Work in pairs. Choose someone in the classroom and tell your partner what he/she looks like. Your partner must try to guess who you are describing.

11   Work in pairs. You are guests at a wedding. Look at the other guests and make comments.

What an extraordinary hat!
What beautiful flowers!

He's got such a big nose!
She's got such long hair!
He's so tall!

12   Work in pairs. You know the following information about the guests.

STUDENT **A**

James Carter is holding hands with the
   doctor's daughter.
Miss Frost is a teacher at the local primary
   school.
The woman with long red hair is Polly Adams.
The miserable-looking man is Arthur Lee.
The tall man with glasses is an accountant.
The woman who's laughing is Jenny O'Brien.

**Copy the chart opposite, and fill in as much
information as you can.
Do not look at Student B's information.**

STUDENT **B**

The man standing by the door is Simon Cash.
Rosie Lee is a student.
The woman with the huge dog is Martha
   Frost.
The handsome man with dark hair is a lawyer.
Beryl Lee smokes cigars.
Major Bray is a Member of Parliament.
The man with the moustache is Pete Smith.

**Copy the chart opposite, and fill in as much
information as you can.
Do not look at Student A's information.**

Guest	Name	Occupation
1		
2		
3		
4		
5		
6		
7		
8		
9		
10		

13 Listen for specific information. Listen to the dialogue and fill in the chart with more information about the guests.

14 Tell each other what you know about the guests. Fill in the rest of the chart.

> Who's the man with the long beard?
> Who's the woman (who's) standing by the table?

> She's the one whose boyfriend is a lawyer.
> He's the man with the big nose.

15 Look at grammar. Fill in the blanks.
Use: *who's* or *whose*

1 He's the man . . . wife is a famous writer.
2 . . . Pete Smith talking to?
3 Rosie Lee's the girl . . . wearing a very short skirt.
4 The woman . . . dog is barking is Martha Frost.
5 The man . . . standing by the table is a Member of Parliament.

16 Write a description of the picture.

Say:
- who all the people are and what they look like
- where they're standing
- what they're doing

17 Role play.
You are a spy. You have to find your partner who is also a spy. But you do not know what he/she looks like. Write a description of yourself with as many details as you like. Finish your description with a password. Choose any noun in this unit as your password.

Give your description to your teacher. You will now receive a description of your partner. Try to guess who wrote it.

When you think you know who your partner is, start a conversation with him/her. Make sure you introduce his/her password into the conversation. If you hear your own password, you have found your partner.

Pronunciation and Structure Review: page 132.

Describing background and experience

1 🔲 **Listen for specific information. Work in pairs. Listen to the conversation between Jean and her colleague Bill.**

STUDENT A

Find out when:

1 Jean was born.
2 her family moved to London.
3 she went to university.
4 she worked as a waitress.
5 she started working as a tourist guide.
6 the travel company offered her a job.

Choose from these dates:

August 1985–July 1986	May 1987
14th August 1964	October 1982
May 1977	October 1986

STUDENT B

Find out when:

7 Jean's father died.
8 she left school.
9 she left university.
10 she got her secretarial diploma.
11 she applied for a job in Barcelona.
12 she arrived in Barcelona.

Choose from these dates:

March 1987	9th June 1987
April 1975	July 1982
June 1985	July 1986

---

2 **Work in pairs. Ask and answer questions to find out when other important events in Jean's life happened.**

When did she . . . ?	On 9th June. In May 1977. Ten years ago. Last week/month/year.

Put the important events and dates of Jean's life in order. Then act out the dialogue between Jean and Bill.

3 **Complete this passage about Jean with the verbs in the list below. Make sure you use the past simple.**

apply   arrive   be (× 2)   decide   die   do
get   go   leave   move   offer   see   start
study   work

Jean O'Hara . . . born in Ireland in 1964. She and her brother Patrick . . . to primary school in Dublin, but their father . . . in 1975, when Jean . . . nearly eleven. Her mother . . . to return to England, and in 1977, the family . . . to London. Jean . . . school in 1982, and . . . Spanish at university for three years. In 1985, she . . . as a waitress while she . . . a secretarial course in English and Spanish. She . . . her diploma in 1986, and that year she . . . working as a tourist guide in London. In March 1987, she . . . an advertisement in the paper for travel representatives in Barcelona, and she . . . for a job. A month ago the travel company . . . her a job starting in June. She . . . in Barcelona last week.

4   Make a list of five important events in your life. Do not write the dates. Then exchange lists with your partner. Ask him/her questions and note down the answers.

Example: – When did you start learning
             English?
           – A year ago./Last year.

5 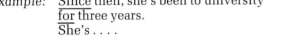 **Listen for main ideas. Listen to the rest of Jean's conversation with Bill. Which of these things has Jean already done since she arrived in Barcelona?**

- found a flat
- climbed the towers of the Sagrada Familia church
- visited the cathedral
- been to the Picasso Museum
- walked along the Rambla
- seen the view of the city from Tibidabo

Say what she has and hasn't done yet. Use the present perfect.

> She hasn't . . . yet.
> She's <u>already</u> . . . .

6   Look at 3 again. Make a list of things that Jean has done since she left school five years ago.

Example: <u>Since</u> then, she's been to university
             <u>for</u> three years.
             She's . . . .

7   Make a list of five important things that have happened in your life in the last five years. Tell your partner what has happened to you, and ask about his/her life.

Example: Since (*year*), I've moved house. My sister has had a baby . . . .

8   Think about your life now. How long have you:

- lived in your present home?
- had your present job?/been at your present school?
- studied English?

Think of two other things you have done for some time. Now ask your partner how long he/she has done things, and answer his/her questions.

Example: I've lived here <u>for</u> ten years.
             I've been at this school <u>since</u> 1986.

9 Look at grammar. Read these news headlines. Write full sentences and change the tense of the verb to the present perfect.

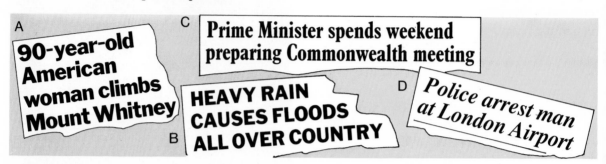

A **90-year-old American woman climbs Mount Whitney**

B **HEAVY RAIN CAUSES FLOODS ALL OVER COUNTRY**

C **Prime Minister spends weekend preparing Commonwealth meeting**

D *Police arrest man at London Airport*

Example: A ninety-year-old American woman has climbed Mount Whitney.

10 Predict before listening. Work in pairs. Which of these words do you expect to hear in each news story? Make four lists.

government	roads	leaders	organised	bank
rivers	cloudy	plane	wind	weather
question	discuss	robbery	Spain	Africa
highest	view	healthy	California	information

11 📼 **Listen for main ideas. Listen to the radio news stories and match them with the headlines. Did you hear the words you expected in each story?**

12 Match the two parts of each sentence and join them using *because*.

The British Government has organised the meeting . . .
People have left their homes . . .
Police have arrested a man at London Airport . . .
A ninety-year-old woman has climbed Mount Whitney twenty-three times . . .

. . . they want to question him about a bank robbery.
. . . it wants to discuss the situation in Africa.
. . . the view from the top is wonderful.
. . . rivers have risen, causing floods.

Example: The British Government has organised the meeting because it wants to discuss the situation in Africa.

Now join the sentences using *so*.

Example: The British Government wants to discuss the situation in Africa, so it has organised the meeting.

13 📼 **Listen to one of the news stories again and try to write it down word for word. You will hear it two or three times. Work with another student when you are ready. Use the outline below to help you.**

A ninety-year-old woman .... At 4418 metres, ... Miss Edna Rogers .... She says the view ...., so .... She also says ....

14 Build your vocabulary. Work in pairs. Talk about your experiences and find out what experience other people have of the following:

mountains	camping	caviar
marathons	horses	musical instruments
cigars	sports cars	English newspapers
diaries	China tea	beards
exams	ghosts	cricket matches

Make questions using the present perfect and these verbs:

play	drive	watch
take	go	run
ride	read	smoke
keep	see	climb
drink	eat	grow

Examples: Have you ever climbed a mountain?
Have you ever been camping?

Have you ever . . . ?	Yes, I have. Yes, (very) often. Yes, once/twice/three times. No, I haven't. No, never.

15 If people have had experience of these things, ask:

- when they did them.
- if they still do them.

Examples: When did you climb a mountain?
Do you <u>still</u> climb mountains?

16 Think about things you have done in your life. Try and find two people in your class who have done at least one of the things you have done.

Tell the rest of the class what you have in common.

Write sentences describing what you have done.

Pronunciation and Structure Review: page 133.

Unit 5 Planning ahead

JULY

2	Monday
3	Tuesday
4	Wednesday
5	Thursday
6	Friday
7	Saturday
8	Sunday

1   Work in pairs.

STUDENT **A**

Look at some of David Piper's arrangements for next week. Copy his diary and fill it in.

Monday 2nd	See Controller Radio 4 3.30 p.m.
Tuesday 3rd	Go to doctor 9 a.m.
Wednesday 4th	Have lunch with Professor Wilson 1 p.m.
Thursday 5th	Meet producers 2–4 p.m.
Friday 6th	Prepare trip to Sri Lanka 9.30 a.m.–1 p.m.

Now tell your partner what David's doing.

Example: He's going to the doctor at nine o'clock on Tuesday morning.

Fill in the rest of the diary with the information your partner tells you. Do not look at your partner's information.

STUDENT **B**

Look at some of David Piper's arrangements for next week. Copy his diary and fill it in.

Monday 2nd	Work in studio 10 a.m.–2 p.m.
Tuesday 3rd	Edit programme 11 a.m.–1 p.m.
Wednesday 4th	Take car to garage 8.30 a.m.
Thursday 5th	Show visitors round Broadcasting House 9.30–11 a.m.
Friday 6th	Interview author 2 p.m.

Fill in the rest of the diary with the information your partner tells you. Do not look at your partner's information.

Now tell your partner what David's doing.

Example: He's working in the studio from ten o'clock to two o'clock on Monday.

---

2 🔲 **Listen for specific information. David is talking to Sally, his production secretary, about more arrangements. Listen and fill in the rest of the diary.**

3 Decide which is the best time for David and Sally to work together. Find out if your partner agrees with you.

4 Write a list of your arrangements for next week. Then think of three more things you would like to do in the company of a friend.

Now work in pairs. Find suitable times to do things you would both like to do. Make excuses and other arrangements if necessary.

> Are you free on . . . ?
> I'm afraid I'm busy on . . .
> I'm (*doing something*).
> I'm free on . . .

5 Predict before listening. Work in pairs. You are going to hear David talking to his wife about his trip to Sri Lanka. Before you listen, which words do you expect to hear?

ambulance	interview	hotel	typewriter	engine
record (v)	photograph (n)	snow	visit	sightseeing

6 Listen for main ideas. Make a rough copy of the map and draw a line to mark David's route.

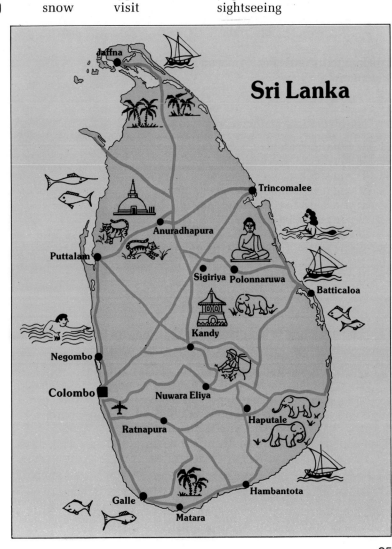

7 Work in pairs. Which things is David going to do?

A   Visit a tea plantation.
B   Stay in a hotel.
C   Have a few days' holiday.
D   Fly to Colombo.
E   Take lots of photographs.
F   Play cricket.
G   Record a programme for *Bookshelf*.
H   Take a guided tour of the island.
I   Write a report on the visit.
J   Interview Arthur C. Clarke.
K   Drive to the hill country.
L   Present a report for a travel programme.

Now listen again and check. As you listen, number the things David is going to do in the order you hear them. Then write a few sentences describing David's plans.

Begin: David <u>is going to</u> fly to Colombo and then he's <u>going to</u> . . .

8 Match the two parts of these statements.

1 If your grandparents die young, . . .
2 If you don't eat sweets, . . .
3 If your parents have dark hair, . . .
4 If you read in bad light, . . .
5 If you take regular exercise, . . .
6 If you eat lots of salad and fresh fruit, . . .
7 If you have a good breakfast, . . .
8 If you eat carrots, . . .
9 If your shoes don't fit properly, . . .

A . . . you'll harm your eyes.
B . . . you won't want to eat between meals.
C . . . you will have a short life as well.
D . . . you won't get heart disease.
E . . . you'll damage your feet.
F . . . your children won't be blonde.
G . . . you'll be able to see in the dark.
H . . . you'll have good teeth.
I . . . you won't catch colds.

**Work in pairs and check your answers. Which
statements are true?**

9 Complete these statements:

1 If you ride a bicycle, . . .
2 If you go out every night, . . .
3 If you smoke, . . .
4 If you read a newspaper every day, . . .
5 If you learn to speak English well, . . .
6 If you go to bed early, . . .
7 If you don't eat enough, . . .
8 If you learn to play an instrument, . . .
9 If you don't save any money, . . .
10 If you travel a lot, . . .

**10 You are going to hear two English teenagers talking about leaving school. First, look at the
statements below. Which ones do you agree with?**

A When you leave school, you'll enjoy life more.
B When you leave school, life will become more complicated.
C As soon as you leave school, you'll have to leave home.
D If you go to university, you won't live at home any more.
E If you go to university, you'll get a better job.
F If you leave school at sixteen, it'll be difficult to get a good job.
G You won't get a university place unless you pass your exams.

when/as soon as	=	it will happen
if	=	it may happen
unless	=	if not

11 📼 Listen for main ideas. Which of the statements in 10 do Angela and Michael agree with?

12 Predict before listening. Here are the interviewer's notes for the second part of the interview. What do you think her questions will be?

	Angela	Michael
Go to university		
Get a job		
Leave home		
Get married		
Have children		
Buy a house		
Stay in England		

13 📼 Listen and check. Write out the interviewer's questions, and make a chart for Angela and Michael as in 12.

14 📼 Listen for main ideas. Fill in your chart for Angela and Michael. Put a tick if they say yes, a cross if they say no, and a question mark if they are not sure.

15 Make true statements about Angela and Michael. Fill in the blanks.
Use: *when if unless* or *as soon as*

Angela:
1   will leave home . . . she goes to university.
2   is going to university . . . she fails her exams.
3   will rent a flat . . . she starts work.
4   will certainly have children . . . she gets married.

Michael:
1   is going to get a job . . . he leaves school.
2   will leave home . . . he gets a job.
3   isn't going to get married . . . he meets the right person.
4   will buy a house . . . he earns enough money.

16 Work in pairs. Think of five things you are going to do in the future if possible. Find out about your partner's plans.

Pronunciation and Structure Review: page 136.

Checking what you know

1 Work in pairs.

STUDENT **A**

Look at the picture. You know four people on the beach.

1 Henry Paul, 35, hairdresser, London.
2 Jenny Bonita, 22, model, Manchester.
3 Peter Rapp, 31, musician, New York.
4 Katy Hughes, 56, writer, Bermuda.

You want to know about the others. Describe them to Student B and find out who they are, how old they are, what they do and where they live. Do not look at Student B's information.

STUDENT **B**

Look at the picture. You know four people on the beach.

5 Joseph Owen, 67, film producer, Los Angeles.
6 Maria da Volvo, 42, actress, Paris.
7 James Tait, 50, businessman, Jersey.
8 Isabel Corazón, 34, journalist, Madrid.

You want to know about the others. Describe them to Student A and find out who they are, how old they are, what they do and where they live. Do not look at Student A's information.

2   Role play. Work in groups of three or four.

GROUP A

Each member of the group plays the role of one of the people 1–4 on the beach. Working together, choose one or two words or phrases from each box below to describe each of your characters, their habits and their relationship to each other.

GROUP B

Each member of the group plays the role of one of the people 5–8 on the beach. Working together, choose one or two words or phrases from each box below to describe each of your characters, their habits and their relationship to each other.

CHARACTER	HABITS	RELATIONSHIPS
charming	smokes cigars	friend
selfish	never stops talking	business colleague
sensitive	always drinks tomato juice	employer
serious	travels a lot	employee
hard-working	wears extraordinary clothes	rival
shy	works at night	husband
bad-tempered	always drinks champagne	wife
proud	drives a Rolls Royce	brother
confident	swims a mile every morning	sister
friendly	doesn't eat meat	son
kind	usually wears sunglasses	daughter

Now meet someone from the other group. Tell him/her about the people you know and find out as much as you can about the people you don't know. Then go back to your groups and discuss what you have found out.

3   Work in pairs.
Think of a job, and mime an action you would do in that job. Do not say what it is! Your partner must try and guess the job by asking questions. Change round when you have finished.

4   Now think of another job. Write a short description of the job.

Describe: • what you have to do in the job
   • qualities needed for the job
   • a typical day

Do not say what the job is. Show your description to your partner.
He/she must guess what the job is.

5   Work in groups.
Imagine you are a famous person. Other students must try to find out who you are by asking questions about your nationality, occupation, place of work, etc. You must try to find out who they are.

6 Work in pairs.

> **STUDENT A**
>
> Look at these photographs very carefully.
> Now choose one of the photographs and ask
> Student B to close his/her book. Ask
> questions about what is happening.

> **STUDENT B**
>
> Look at these photographs very carefully.
> Student A is going to ask you to close your
> book and answer questions about what is
> happening in one of them.

When you have finished, change roles and choose another picture.

A

B

C

7 Listen for specific information. Work in pairs. Listen to David talking about his life.

> **STUDENT A**
>
> **Find out:**
> 1 when he started teaching.
> 2 when he worked in Rome.
> 3 how long he and Annette stayed in Rio.
> 4 when their daughter was born.
> 5 when he started working for BBC English
>   by Radio and Television.
> 6 when he joined BBC Radio 4.

> **STUDENT B**
>
> **Find out:**
> 7 where he met Annette.
> 8 when they got married.
> 9 when they went to Rio.
> 10 when they returned to London.
> 11 when their son was born.
> 12 how long David has been at BBC Radio 4.

8 Work in pairs. Ask and answer questions to find out when other important events in David's
life happened.
Write your answers in sentences. Then put the twelve sentences in order and write a short
description of David's life.

9 Work in groups of four or five. You are going to play a game called BEAT THAT!
Your teacher is going to give each group a sentence, such as 'I've seen David Bowie.'
The first player changes the verb: 'I've *met* David Bowie.'
The second player changes any other part of the sentence except 'I': 'I've met *Mick Jagger*.'
The third player changes the verb again: 'I've *had lunch with* Mick Jagger.'
The fourth player changes any other part of the sentence except 'I': 'I've had lunch with *David Bowie and* Mick Jagger.'
The game continues until a player says something that the next player cannot beat, and scores one point. At the end of the game, the player with the highest number of points is the winner.

10 Listen for main ideas. Robert is telling his parents what he is going to do in Scotland. Listen and follow the route.

11 Work in pairs. Ask and say what Robert will do:

- if it stays fine
- if it rains
- when he gets to Inverness
- if he gets a lift in a car
- if he can't get a lift
- if he hasn't got enough money

Example: — What'll he do if it stays fine?
— He'll sleep in his tent.

Now write a description of Robert's tour of Scotland.

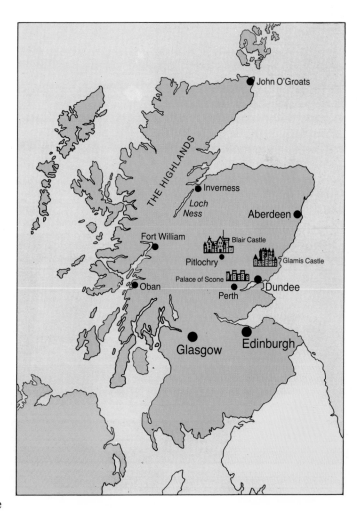

12 Ask your partner questions about his/her life, and note down the answers.

Find out:

- where and when he/she was born
- where he/she went to school
- if he/she has been to university/college
- what jobs he/she has had
- how long he/she has had the present job
- where he/she lives now, and how long he/she has lived there
- what his/her future plans are

Now write a short description of your partner's life. Use the passage on page 20 to help you. Then exchange your written work with your partner, and check your own biography.

13 Build your vocabulary. Look back over Units 1 to 5 and write five words in each of the categories below.

FAMILY   JOBS   PERSONAL QUALITIES
PERSONAL APPEARANCE

Talking about present interests and past events

1   Think of three things you like doing, and three things you don't like doing.

I	love like enjoy 'm not keen on don't like hate	—ing. —ing . . .

Examples: I love going to the theatre.
I'm not keen on dancing.

Now find someone in your class who likes the same things as you. Say why you like or don't like doing things.

2   Work in pairs. The photographs below show some of the things Robert likes doing. Choose from this list and say what he likes doing.

sightseeing
playing football
dancing
going to the cinema
watching television
visiting museums and
   galleries
eating in restaurants

listening to music
playing tennis
walking
going to the theatre
reading
running
travelling

3 ▣ Listen for main ideas. Look at the list in 2, and listen to Robert's conversation with Annie. What else do you think he likes doing? What do you think he doesn't like doing? Check your answers with your partner.

4 Read for specific information. Look at this brochure on things to do in Edinburgh. Which things will Robert want to do in Edinburgh?

[cassette] **Now listen and check.**

5 Work in pairs. Which places in Edinburgh would you like to visit? Tell your partner why.

6 Complete the dialogue.

Use:
- I don't really like
- I'd rather
- I'd love to
- Why don't we
- How about

ANNIE:	. . . go to a concert tomorrow evening?
ROBERT:	I'm afraid . . . going to concerts. . . . go to the theatre.
ANNIE:	But there isn't anything worth seeing at the moment. . . . going to the cinema?
ROBERT:	Hey, that's a great idea. . . . !

[cassette] **Listen and check.**

7 Work in pairs and make invitations to do things in Edinburgh. Use the dialogue in 6 to help you.

Would you like to go . . . ? Why don't we go . . . ? How about going . . . ?	Yes, I'd love to. That's a good idea! All right. I'd rather . . . I'm sorry, I can't. I'm afraid I don't like . . .

EDINBURGH ZOO

Visit Scotland's largest animal collection with over 2000 animals in 70 acres of attractive gardens. All the family's animal favourites are here and first-class restaurants, shops and play areas make Edinburgh Zoo a great day out for all ages.

EDINBURGH CASTLE

This most famous of Scottish castles dates from the Norman period. See the crown jewels of Scotland and the famous 15th century gun 'Mons Meg'. Car parking available. Open Monday–Saturday 9.30 a.m.–5.05 p.m., Sunday 11 a.m.–5.05 p.m.

PALACE OF HOLYROOD HOUSE

Ticket office open weekdays for guided tours 9.30 a.m.–5.15 p.m., Sundays 10.30 a.m.–4.30 p.m. Closed 12th–27th May, 14th July–4th August, when occupied by the Queen; and occasionally other times. Tour normally includes State Rooms with 17th and 18th century furniture, tapestries and paintings, and apartments where Mary Queen of Scots lived.

LEITH-SUR-MER

Look into the historic Port of Leith, home of golf, fine waterfront restaurants and wine bars. There's even one on a boat! Sample Leith claret before visiting our festival theatre. All this, close to the city centre, at the end of a scenic riverside walkway.

KING'S THEATRE

Edinburgh's main theatre has a packed annual programme, which includes top companies such as the National Theatre, comedies and musicals, one-night stands and the traditional Christmas pantomime. For programme and box office details tel: 031-229 1201.

MEADOWBANK

Scotland's foremost leisure centre is internationally famous as a Commonwealth Games venue, but everyone can use its super facilities. Equipment can be hired for most sports and activities, and there is an excellent cafeteria overlooking the stadium.

ROYAL MUSEUM OF SCOTLAND

See 'Scotland through the Ages'. Exhibits range from prehistoric times through to the days of Bonnie Prince Charlie and beyond into the 1890s. Sculptured stones, Scottish coins and medals, weapons, costume, Roman objects, silver and pewter. Open Monday–Saturday 10 a.m–5 p.m., Sunday 2 p.m.–5 p.m. Admission free. Tel: 031-557 3550.

8 Work in groups. Write a guide list of things to see and do in your town. For each place or entertainment in your guide, say:
- where it is or where it's on
- when it opens and closes or starts and finishes
- why it's worth seeing

9 Now make and accept or refuse invitations to do things every day next week. Use your town guide for ideas.

10 **Predict before reading. The passage below is about the Edinburgh International Festival of Music, Drama and Art. Which of the following words do you expect to see in it?**

band	entertainment	exhibition
shopping	church	damage
dentist	perform	boat
choice	audience	crowds
event	films	vegetable
match	mountain	dancers

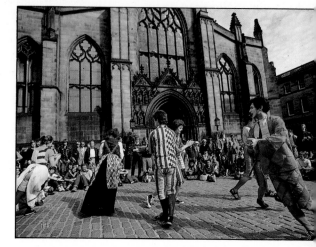

11 **Read for specific information.**

Find out: • when the festival is
• when it began
• what kinds of entertainment it offers

Suddenly one Sunday in August, the streets are filled with colour. A procession of bands, dancers, jugglers and trick cyclists makes its way slowly through the city. Every evening, crowds of people walk up to the top of the Royal Mile, looking forward to a display of military music. On every shop window and noticeboard, posters have appeared, advertising everything from poetry readings to children's theatre, art exhibitions to concerts. It's festival time.

From its beginning in 1947, the Edinburgh International Festival (the 'official' festival) has become a world-famous cultural event. The city turns into a giant arts centre, with its music, drama, dance and exhibitions, all by artistes of international fame. Every year more than twenty nations perform to audiences from all over the world in theatres, halls, schools, churches and the streets of the city. The Edinburgh Military Tattoo adds to the choice of entertainment, with its display of marching and military bands in Edinburgh Castle.

The Festival Fringe (the 'unofficial' festival) is the biggest event of its kind in the world, with more than 900 shows to choose from and over 6000 writers and performers taking part. It gives visitors and residents a first-class opportunity to see many works performed for the first time—several of which go on to successful performances elsewhere.

The Film Festival gives fans an opportunity to widen their knowledge of films. And to show that there is something for everyone, the Jazz Festival has become very popular in recent years. You can hear the very best of music all over the city at this time.

There is no more exciting place to be than in Edinburgh at Festival time!

Check your answers with another student.

12 **Deal with difficult vocabulary. Look at these sentences from the passage. Decide what type of word (noun, adjective, verb) is missing.**

1 The Edinburgh International Festival has become a world-famous cultural . . . .
2 Every year more than twenty nations . . . in theatres, halls, schools, churches and the streets of the city.
3 The Festival Fringe (the 'unofficial' . . .) is the . . . event of its kind in the world.
4 The Film Festival gives . . . an opportunity to . . . their knowledge of films.
5 And to show that there is something for everyone, the Jazz Festival has become very . . . in recent years.

Now think of a word to complete the sentences. Check your answers with another student. Then look at the passage and check.

13 Build your vocabulary. Find words in the passage in 11 which refer to:

- the performers
- the places they perform in
- the people they perform to
- the things they perform

Check your answers with another student.

14 Look at this programme of some of the events at the Edinburgh Festival.

National Youth Music Theatre: *Let's Make an Opera* by Benjamin Britten

Stary Theatre of Krakow: *Crime and Punishment* by Dostoyevsky

Lyon Opera Ballet: *Cinderella* by Prokofiev

BBC Symphony Orchestra: *Piano Concerto No 5* by Beethoven, *Alpine Symphony* by Strauss

The Glenlivet Fireworks Concert

Scottish Art Today: *Artists at Work – 1986*

Rowan Atkinson: *The New Revue*

Cambridge Footlights: *Another Fine Mess*, Footlights 1986 Revue

Edinburgh Puppet Company: *Rama and Sita/Rumpelstiltskin*

Bert Jansch and Paul Millns: In Concert

Oxford Theatre Group: *The Elephant Man* by Bernard Pomerance

Fringe Sunday: The Fringe's Open Day in Holyrood Park. Sixty different acts will give twenty-minute selections from their shows.

▣ Now listen for main ideas. Listen to a woman and a man talking to a reporter about the Festival. Which things in the programme have they seen or done?

15 ▣ Listen again and note down:

- how long the two people have been in Edinburgh
- how many times they've been to the Festival
- what else they've done during their stay

Compare your notes with another student.
Then write a few sentences about what the two people have done.

Examples: She's been in Edinburgh <u>for</u> a week. She's <u>just</u> been to a concert, but she hasn't seen any exhibitions <u>yet</u>.
He's been there <u>since</u> Sunday. He's <u>already</u> been to six shows today.

16 Work in groups. Add some more entertainments to the town guide you made in 8. Use your guide to find out what other students have or haven't done in the town.

Pronunciation and Structure Review: page 138.

Unit 8 — Saying how you feel

1 Build your vocabulary.
Look at these words to describe feelings. Which words do you know?

lonely	nervous
tired	sad
angry	depressed
upset	bored
surprised	excited
happy	pleased
annoyed	frightened
amused	worried

Ask your partner about words you do not understand.

2
Look at the photograph of Jean and say how you think she feels. Choose from the adjectives in 1.

She looks	very . . . . quite/rather . . . . a little/a bit . . . .

3 ▣ Listen for main ideas.
Listen to the conversation between Jean and her colleague Isabel. Look at the adjectives in 1 and write down the ones you hear.
Now ask and say how Jean feels and why.

Example: — How does Jean feel?
— She's depressed because she hasn't found a flat yet.

4 ▣ Listen for specific information.
Listen again. Which of these expessions do you hear?

Oh, I *am* sorry!	Oh really?
Oh dear!	That's great!
What a nuisance!	That's nice!
What a surprise!	How marvellous!
What a pity!	How awful!

5
Read the sentences below and choose a suitable reaction from the expressions in 4.

1 I can't sleep properly.
2 My father's not very well.
3 I can't find my passport.
4 The airline's lost my suitcase.
5 I don't believe it – it's Jean O'Hara!

▣ **Now listen to Jean's reactions, and check.**

6 Work in pairs. Look at these pictures. Say how you think the people feel.

Example: She looks amus<u>ed</u>.

What has made them feel like this? They are reacting to the things in these pictures. Decide what has caused each person's reaction.

Why does . . . feel	amus<u>ed</u>? exci<u>ted</u>? bo<u>red</u>? frigh<u>tened</u>?	Because he/she thinks . . . is	amus<u>ing</u>. exci<u>ting</u>. bo<u>ring</u>. frigh<u>tening</u>.

7 Work in pairs. Ask and say what makes you feel:

- angry
- bored
- frightened
- excited
- happy
- depressed

- annoyed
- upset
- sad
- tired
- amused
- worried

8 Find out how other students react to things. Then write sentences describing how they feel.

Examples: Monday mornings make Jacques depressed.
Yuko feels annoyed when people smoke in the cinema.
Bjørn thinks Woody Allen is very amusing.

37

9 Predict before listening. Work in pairs. You are going to listen to a story called 'The House on the Hill'. It is in four parts. The words below belong to the first part. Try to guess what happens in the first part.

Mr White .... car .... Penny White .... thanks .... help ....

.... father .... left .... new house .... lonely .... nearest town .... miles ....

.... phone .... dead .... frightened .... noise .... wind .... rain .... bed ....

.... tired .... asleep .... woke .... dark .... noise ....

**Now listen and check.
Did you guess correctly?**

10 Predict before listening. Here are some phrases from the second part of the story. Try to guess what happens in this part.

It was the postman
There's no Mr Parker here
ten years since anyone lived here
Was he the last owner?
I'm new here
ask the neighbour for his new address
She took the letters and went inside
It was the milkman
didn't order any milk
doorbell rang a third time
got a parcel here, for . . . for . . .
looked like a suitcase
IMPORTANT: TO WAIT FOR MR PARKER

**Now listen and check.
Did you guess correctly?**

11   Read and predict. Read the third part of the story and fill in the blanks.

The House on the Hill

PART THREE

The rain fell and the wind blew as Penny . . . to the neighbour's house. An old woman . . . . She looked annoyed by Penny's visit. 'Hello', said Penny. 'I live in the house on the hill.'

'In the Parker house?' Mrs Lane asked.

'That's right. Do you know . . . ? I've got some things for him.'

The old lady looked at Penny. 'You'd better come in,' she said. Penny took off . . . and sat down. 'You know about Mr Parker then, do you?' asked Mrs Lane. Penny said no. 'Oh. A sad story. He was a sailor. He lived most of his life at sea. He only came . . . every ten years. But the last time he came back, there was someone living in his house, a stranger. Mr Parker was very angry.'

'What happened?' asked Penny.

'There was an awful fight. The stranger . . . , in his own house.'

Penny asked 'When did this happen?'

The old lady replied 'Let me see now, oh, about . . . .' She looked at Penny. '. . . ?' she asked.

Penny replied, 'From London.'

'So you're a stranger as well,' Mrs Lane said.

It was dark as Penny walked home. She was rather worried by . . . . The rain fell and the wind blew.

🔊 Listen and check. How does the story make you feel?

12   Predict before listening. Try to guess what happens in the last part of the story.

🔊 Now listen and check. Did you guess correctly?

13   Write out the whole story in exactly fifty words.

Pronunciation and Structure Review: page 139.

Doing the right thing

1 Read for main ideas. These sentences are from a travel guide to Sri Lanka. Match the sentences with the following paragraph headings:

SHOPPING
LUGGAGE
CLOTHING
HEALTH
TIPPING
MONEY

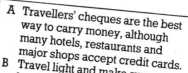

A Travellers' cheques are the best way to carry money, although many hotels, restaurants and major shops accept credit cards.

B Travel light and make sure you leave some room in your suitcase for souvenirs.

C However, you may pay less if you have cash.

D Jewellery, brassware, ivory and woodcarvings make popular souvenirs.

E Don't drink the tap water in Sri Lanka unless you know it has been boiled. It's safe to drink the water in most of the big hotels; elsewhere we recommend drinking bottled water.

F Make sure you take some woollen clothes if you're going to the hill country, where temperatures drop sharply at night.

G It's a good idea to take an empty bag for those extra items that you can't resist.

H Ask your doctor to give you some pills for stomach upsets.

I Even on cloudy days the sun can be dangerous in Sri Lanka if aren't careful.

J Basketware, leather goods a cotton shirts and trousers are a good buy.

K Use a sun-cream and wear a l

L Never accept the first price a shopkeeper suggests; bargai can be fun!

M Porters expect a tip of about 3 4 rupees per bag.

N Eat fruit only when it's peeled a beware of green salad.

O Imported medicines are very expensive, so if you have to take something special, bring a supp with you.

P Hotels and restaurants usually add a service charge of about 10 per cent to the bill.

Q If in doubt, drink hot tea, or the water from the king coconut.

R In the coastal regions, only light tropical clothing is comfortable. Don't forget to pack a pair of sandals for sightseeing.

S A good insect spray is useful.

T During the rainy season, you will need a raincoat and an umbrella.

2 Build your vocabulary. Look at the passage and find:

- two kinds of luggage
- three types of drink
- two types of food
- three items of clothing
- three kinds of money

3 Work in pairs. Look at the equipment. Decide which things David should take on his trip and say why they are necessary.

He	ought to should needs to	take . . . because . . . .

Now say why he doesn't need to take the other things.

He	doesn't need to doesn't have to	take . . . because . . . .

4  Listen for specific information. David is asking a friend about what he should take on a trip. Listen and check your answers to 3.

5 Read for specific information. Look at the passage in 1 and say if there is anything else David needs to take. Say why.

6 Predict before listening. David has some more questions. Look at his notes. What do you think he's going to ask?

Example: What can I do to avoid stomach upsets?

- stomach upsets
- things to buy
- medicines
- clothes
- money
- tipping

7 Listen and check.
Listen to David's questions again, and answer them. Use the passage in 1 to help you.

Example: – What can I do to avoid stomach upsets?
– You shouldn't eat fruit unless it's peeled, and you ought to drink only bottled or boiled water.

Don't forget to . . . You'd better . . . You ought/oughtn't . . . You should/shouldn't . . .

8 Write sentences giving advice to people visiting your country. Give advice on:

- what clothes they should bring
- how they should pay bills
- what medicines they ought to bring
- if they need to give tips to waiters
- what things they ought to buy

Use the passage in 1 to help you.

41

9 Work in pairs. Look at the situations below and discuss what advice you would give to Pam, Brian, Janet and Alan.

Pam Her fourteen-year-old daughter often steals money from her handbag. Pam has a part-time job in the evenings, and her husband is a long-distance lorry-driver.

Brian He is an unemployed engineer. His home is on Merseyside, and so are all his friends. But he's had a job offer in Aberdeen, 575 km away.

Janet She owns a small restaurant in London. The restaurant is successful, and Janet is very proud of it. She has just heard that her husband has to work in Canada for three years for his company.

Alan He wants to marry his nineteen-year-old girlfriend. She is in love with him too, but her parents are against the marriage. He's eighteen and about to go to college.

10 📼 Listen for main ideas. The people in 9 phoned the radio programme *What's the Problem?* to ask for advice. Listen and decide which advice was given to each person.

(Your address)

(The date)

Dear *(first name)*,
It was very good to hear from you and to know that you are enjoying your new job. But I'm sorry that you're feeling lonely.

(Give advice)

I'm sure you'll get to know people soon. Do write again and let me know how you're getting on.

Love,
(Your first name)

11 📼 Listen for specific information. Look at the sentences below, and find the two pieces of advice for each person in 9. Be careful! There is some extra advice.

A Find out what he really wants to do.
B Invite them round to talk about it.
C Accept the job offer.
D Tell the police.
E Leave your husband.
F Wait a couple of years.
G Look for a daytime job.
H Turn down the job offer.
I Tell her that you know about it.
J Find someone to run the restaurant.
K Get married as soon as possible.
L Keep in touch with your family and friends.

Do you agree with the advice on the radio programme? Was your advice similar?

12 Write two sentences giving advice to each person. Make sure you use the structures you have learnt in this unit.

13 Write a letter giving advice to a close friend who has left his/her home town to work in a big city. He/she is enjoying the new job, but feels very lonely. Give advice on how to get to know people. Use the outline letter to help you.

14 Read and connect ideas. Read the passage and decide where these sentences should go.

A What a lovely dog you have!
B suggests a different route
C Can I buy anyone a drink
D why the English love dogs so much
E because they are rather shy
F Yes, it's much too hot
G no one agrees about the weather in England

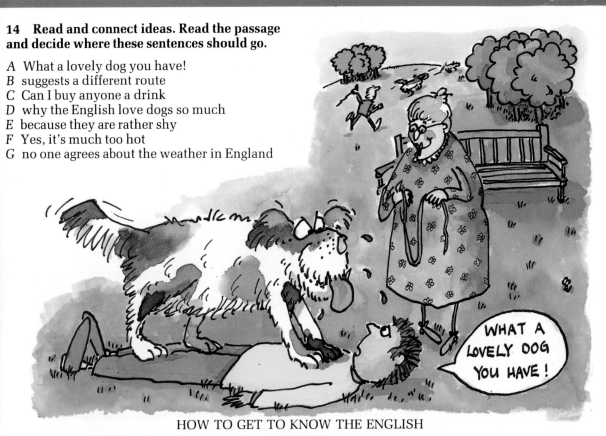

HOW TO GET TO KNOW THE ENGLISH

It is often said that the English are cold and unfriendly, but in fact this is . . . . If you are a foreigner, there are a number of ways to get to know the English. For example, imagine you are in a park where there are lots of people with their dogs. Now, you can't say to someone, 'What beautiful hair you have!' even if it's true. But you can say, '. . . .' This is a very good way to start a conversation, even if the dog isn't lovely at all. In fact, this is probably . . . . And who knows how the conversation will end?

Another way is to stand at the bus stop and say 'What extraordinary weather we're having.' Remember that everyone thinks the weather in England is extraordinary. The other person will say '. . . ,' if it's sunny, or 'Yes, it's wonderful for the garden,' if it's pouring with rain. Then, anyone who is listening will disagree, because . . . . After five minutes you've made lots of friends (and a few enemies as well, but never mind).

Another good trick is to stand on a street corner with a map looking lost. After only two or three minutes, someone comes up to you and gives you directions. Sometimes, two or more people offer their help. Everyone . . . because no one knows how to get there or even where you are at the moment. But that's not the point. The point is to get to know the English, not to find the way. After all, you've got a map for that.

But the best way is to walk into a pub and ask in a loud voice, '. . . ?' This is the universal way to get to know people. Of course, it's quite expensive, but you can't put a price on friends. Can you?

15 Read for main ideas. Read the passage again. Then write sentences describing the things you should do to get to know the English.

16 Work in pairs. Discuss the things you should do to get to know people in your country/countries.

Pronunciation and Structure Review: page 141.

Talking about the past

1   Look at these photographs. Say what Robert was doing at these times: 11 a.m., 1 p.m., 4 p.m., 7 p.m. Choose from this list:

He was having a drink.
He was having lunch.
He was visiting the National Gallery of Scotland.
He was standing outside a cinema.
He was walking down a famous street, the
    Royal Mile.
He was sitting in a museum.
He was waiting for a bus.

2   Work in pairs. Look at Annie's diary. Ask and say what she was doing at the same times as Robert.

Example: – What was Annie doing at 11 a.m.?
                     – She was seeing her boss.

9.15 a.m.	Meet client
10 a.m.	Talk to Henry about work
11 a.m.	See boss
12 noon	Phone bank manager
1 p.m.	Have lunch with Susie
1.45 p.m.	Go to bank
2.30 p.m.	Visit head office
3.30 p.m.	Look at house
4 p.m.	Write report
7 p.m.	Leave flat (Meet Robert at cinema – film starts 7.30)

3   Make sentences about Robert and Annie using *while*.

While Robert was (*doing something*), Annie was (*doing something else*).

Robert was (*doing something*) while Annie was (*doing something else*).

4   Work in pairs. Ask and say what Annie was doing at the other times.

5   Work in pairs. Ask and say what you were doing at these times:

● yesterday
● last week

Example: – What were you doing at 9.15 yesterday morning?
                     – I was reading a newspaper.

6 Look at the photographs and match the two parts of each sentence using *when*. Say what Annie was doing.

She was washing her hair		her bus went past.
She was leaving the house	when	the phone rang.
She was walking to the bus stop		it started to rain.
She was waiting for the bus		a friend arrived.

7 Look at grammar. Now make sentences using *while*.

Example: While she was leaving the house,
              a friend arrived.

      or

              A friend arrived while she was leaving
              the house.

8 Look at grammar. Read the dialogue and fill in the blanks. Use *while* where you can. Otherwise use *when*.

ROBERT: Annie! There you are!

ANNIE: Robert, I'm so sorry I'm late.

ROBERT: What happened?

ANNIE: Oh, well, I got home from work quite late, because so many people were phoning us all afternoon. It was incredible. I was feeling very tired . . . I got back. And then, . . . I was washing my hair, the phone rang – it was my mother.

ROBERT: So you had a long conversation.

ANNIE: Yes – she was still telling me her news half an hour later . . . I had to leave for the cinema. Well, I was leaving the house . . . my friend Patti arrived. She's just finished with her boyfriend, and she's very upset, so I had to spend ten minutes with her.

ROBERT: Oh, I'm sorry.

ANNIE: Then, I was walking to the bus stop . . . my bus went past. I was so annoyed! Just for once it was early and I missed it! And then . . . I was waiting for the next bus, it started to rain, so I ran back to get my umbrella. Of course, . . . I was going back home, the rain stopped. I'm sorry, Robert. Are we too late for the film?

ROBERT: Never mind – we can see it some other time. Let's go and have something to eat.

▶◀ Now listen and check.

45

9 Think of excuses for these situations.

- You haven't done your English homework.
- You arrived late at your English class today.
- You had a minor accident while driving your friend's car.
- You've forgotten your best friend's birthday.
- You've had a large meal in a restaurant, and you haven't enough money to pay the bill.

Now go round the class. Ask for and make excuses for the situations.

Example: – Why haven't you done your homework?
– Because I was practising my English conversation with a very nice Englishman/woman last night.

Which were the best excuses in the class?

11 Listen for detail. Listen to a radio news version of the same story. Note any differences.

Examples:

NEWSPAPER	RADIO
Parisian burglar	French burglar
house	flat

Now work in pairs and discuss the differences between the two versions.

Example: In the newspaper it said he was a Parisian burglar, but on the radio it said he was a French burglar.

10 Read and connect ideas. The story below is from a newspaper. Put the sections of the story in the right order.

A He was feeling rather hungry so he ate a piece. He was looking round the rest of the house, stealing jewellery and paintings, when he began to feel rather thirsty.

B He was still feeling thirsty so he drank a second bottle. And a third.

C Next morning when the owners got home, he was still lying on the bed, fast asleep. He only woke up when the police arrived and arrested him.

D A Parisian burglar broke into a house while the owners were away for the weekend. While he was looking for things to steal, he found some of his favourite cheese in the kitchen.

E He went back to the kitchen where he found some champagne. He drank the whole bottle.

F A little later, while he was taking things from the bedroom, he began to feel tired. So he lay on the bed, just for a few minutes.

Now check your answers with another student.

12   Predict before listening. Work in pairs.
Look at the pictures which illustrate a story.
They are in the wrong order. Try to guess what
the story is about and put the pictures in the
right order.

**13   Predict before listening. Here are some phrases from the story. What do you think
happens in the story?**

Jack Grant was driving to London
began to feel rather tired
stopped the car at the side of the road
drinking his coffee
knocked on the window
asked him the time
closed his eyes and went to sleep
Jack told him it was a quarter to eight

rather annoyed
wrote a note and put it on the windscreen
went back to sleep
sleeping heavily
policeman came up to the car
read the note
woke Jack up

14   Listen and check. Did you guess correctly?
Now write the story out. Use the phrases in 13, and linking words: *and   so   then   when   while*

15   Work in pairs. Prepare a description of a day when everything went wrong for you.
Now tell the others about your disastrous day!

Pronunciation and Structure Review: page 142.

11 Facing the facts

1 Read and predict. Jean has booked a table in a restaurant for a party of twelve people. Read the dialogue and decide where these phrases and sentences should go.

- Well, I want to speak to
- I'm afraid
- There's nothing I can do.
- That's all right.
- I understand what's happened.
- It's our fault. I do apologise.
- I'm terribly sorry
- But that's impossible!
- I'm sorry, but
- I'd like to make a complaint.

WAITER:	Good evening, madam.
JEAN:	Good evening. I've booked a table for nine o'clock.
WAITER:	Can I have your name, please?
JEAN:	Miss O'Hara.
WAITER:	O'Hara . . . we have no reservation in your name.
JEAN:	. . . I phoned yesterday and booked a table for twelve.
WAITER:	. . . the restaurant is full. . . .
JEAN:	. . . someone who can do something.
MANAGER:	What's the problem, madam?
JEAN:	. . . I've booked a table for this evening, and apparently the restaurant is full.
MANAGER:	. . . , madam. The restaurant is full this evening. You can have a table tomorrow evening.
JEAN:	That's no good. I've got a party of twelve people and they're flying home tomorrow.
MANAGER:	What was your name again?
JEAN:	O'Hara.
MANAGER:	Ah, . . . You do have a reservation after all.
JEAN:	Really?
MANAGER:	Yes, you're down as Miss Harlow. . . . . . .
JEAN:	. . . It was a bad line when I telephoned.
MANAGER:	Please come this way.

Listen and check.

2 Role play. Work in groups of three. Act out the role play using the phrases in 1.

STUDENT A

Your name is Parker, and you have booked a room for tonight at the Hotel Miró. It's late and you don't want to stay anywhere else.

STUDENT B

You are the receptionist at the Hotel Miró. You have no reservation in the name of Parker, and the hotel is full. You ring for the manager.

STUDENT C

You are the manager of the Hotel Miró. You ask what the problem is. Apologise to the customer and ask for his/her name. There is a reservation in the name of Barker.

---

3 Listen for main ideas. You are going to hear three people complaining by telephone. What is each person complaining about?

4 Complete part of dialogue 1 below with suitable phrases from this list.

- I bought it (*say when*). I've got the receipt.
- Yes, I'd like to make a complaint about (*an item*) I bought in your shop.
- There is sound, but there's no picture.
- Thank you very much.
- It's stopped.
- It doesn't work.
- I washed it, and it shrank.

ASSISTANT:	Good morning, this is the clock department. Can I help you?
CUSTOMER:	. . . .
ASSISTANT:	What's wrong with it?
CUSTOMER:	. . . .
ASSISTANT:	How long have you had it?
CUSTOMER:	. . . .
ASSISTANT:	Well, bring it back and we'll replace it for you.
CUSTOMER:	. . . .

Listen and check.

5 Work in groups of three and act out dialogue 1. Use the phrases in 4 and the telephone phrases below to help you.

YOU HEAR	YOU SAY
Good morning/afternoon, this is (*name of shop*). Hold the line, please. This is (*person/department*) speaking.	Could I speak to (*person/department*)? Can you put me through to (*person/department*)?
OR	
I'm afraid he's/she's not available at the moment. I'm afraid the line's engaged. Can I take a message? Can I ask him/her to call you back?	Could I leave a message? Can you ask him/her to call me back, please? I'll try again later.
Goodbye.	Goodbye.

Change roles and partners, and act out dialogues 2 and 3.

6 Look at the pictures below and match them with the following statements.

1 You've broken it.
2 You're very late.
3 Oh no! You forgot to turn off the oven.
4 You were driving too fast.

7 Predict before listening. For each situation in 6, decide which of the following excuses is most likely.

A I'm sorry – I was having lunch with a friend and I forgot the time.
B I'm terribly sorry – I didn't realise. I was trying to get to the station.
C I am sorry – I dropped it while I was making the coffee.
D I'm afraid so – I was watching a fascinating programme on TV.

📼 **Listen and check.**

8 Look at grammar. Study these sentences.

Jean is Irish, isn't she?

You speak Spanish, don't you?

They missed the plane, didn't they?

Bill's got a car, hasn't he?

Now choose from the question tags below, and complete each of the statements in 6.

● weren't you?   ● aren't you?
● haven't you?   ● don't you
● isn't it?   ● didn't you?

📼 **Listen again and check. Then practise the exchanges with a partner.**

9 Role play. There has been a burglary. The police have arrested a person with a suitcase containing:

- a pair of nylon stockings
- two metres of rope
- a screwdriver
- a torch
- a pair of gloves
- £2000 in bank notes

At the police station, the suspect has to explain the contents of the suitcase. Work in pairs.

STUDENT A

You are a policeman/policewoman.

Ask Student B to explain why these things were in the suitcase.

Example: What's this? It's a piece of rope, isn't it?

STUDENT B

You are the suspect.

Make good excuses to explain why you were carrying these things.

Example: Yes, but it's not what you think, officer. I was helping a friend – his car broke down.

---

10 Read and connect ideas. The sentences on the left give the first part of six stories. The second parts of the stories are on the right. Match the two parts of each story.

1 Sylvia Weston was making a pot of tea when a bus drove into her house.
2 Archimedes was having a bath when he made a very important discovery.
3 Roger Mallon was walking along the roof of a high speed train when the police arrested him.
4 Doris Miles was walking away from a shoe shop in a new pair of shoes when the shop owner caught her.
5 Jenny Walsh was watching the news on TV when she saw a report that her house was on fire.
6 Peter Goodchild was climbing down a chimney when the police found him.

A He explained, 'I was visiting a friend, and I couldn't find the front door.'
B She filled a bucket with water, and poured it over the television.
C She poured out a cup and offered it to the shocked driver.
D He told the police, 'I had a second class ticket, and I was looking for the bar.'
E He immediately shouted 'Eureka!' and jumped out of the bath.
F She said, 'I only wanted to see what they looked like in daylight.'

11 Work in pairs. Check your answers with your partner by asking and answering questions about the stories.

Examples: – What was Sylvia Weston doing when a bus drove into her house?
    – She was making a pot of tea.

    – What did she do when the bus drove into her house?
    – She poured out a cup and offered it to the shocked driver.

12 Work in groups of four or five. Tell other students about an important event in your life.
Say: • what you were doing when it happened
    • what you did when it happened

Example: I'll never forget the day my exam results arrived. I was having breakfast when I got the letter. I was so nervous that I had to ask my mother to open it.

Now write about what happened to three people in your group. Write a couple of sentences about each event, as in the stories in 10.

Pronunciation and Structure Review: page 144.

12 Checking what you know

1   Work in pairs. Read through the questionnaire, then ask your partner questions.

Examples: Are you very logical?
Do you enjoy dancing and listening to music?

Note down your partner's answers, and answer questions about yourself.

ARE YOU A LEFT BRAIN OR A RIGHT BRAIN THINKER?

We now know that the left side of the brain 'thinks' differently from the right side. Of course, we all use both sides of the brain, but most people use one side more than the other. 'Left brain' people are usually logical, and find it easy to express themselves in words. They are often good at mathematics. 'Right brain' people are usually artistic and imaginative. They often understand things immediately without following a logical path.

Opposite, you will find twenty statements to which you answer 'Yes' or 'No'. If the statement is true for you, answer 'Yes'. If the statement is not at all like you, answer 'No'.

1 You are very logical.
2 You enjoy dancing and listening to music.
3 You'd rather find out all the facts before you make a decision.
4 Your dreams at night are real and very alive.
5 You are good at drawing outlines and plans.
6 You often say or do things without thinking about the consequences.
7 You can speak a few words in several languages.
8 You are often late because you forget what time it is.
9 You can usually describe your feelings.
10 You often make decisions based on feelings rather than facts.
11 You are very tidy and organised.
12 Sometimes you have the feeling you've seen something or been somewhere in another life.
13 You are good at giving directions and explaining things.
14 Colours are important to you, in clothes, etc.
15 You are usually patient in difficult situations.
16 You are sensitive and you get upset easily.
17 You're keen on puzzles and word games.
18 You love beautiful things.
19 You like solving problems.
20 You enjoy luxury.

HOW TO SCORE

Count the number of 'Yes' answers to the odd-numbered statements (1, 3, 5, 7, 9, 11, 13, 15, 17, 19) and write it down. These statements are typical of 'left brain' thinkers.
Now count the number of 'Yes' answers to the even-numbered statements (2, 4, 6, 8, 10, 12, 14, 16, 18, 20) and write it down. These statements are typical of 'right brain' thinkers.
If both scores are more or less the same, then you probably use both sides of the brain equally. If one score is much higher than the other, then you use that side of the brain most often.

2 Write a short paragraph about your partner using his/her answers to the questionnaire.

Example: Ari is often late because he forgets what time it is.

Does your partner agree with your description?

3 Find another student whose results in the questionnaire are similar to yours. Ask each other questions to find three things you both like doing, and three things you both dislike doing.

Examples: Do you like dancing?
Do you enjoy travelling?

4 Work in pairs. Ask and say how you feel when:

A you see someone smoking in a NO SMOKING area
B you take off in a plane
C you visit someone in hospital
D you watch horror films
E it's raining
F you're waiting for someone who's late
G you have no work to do
H you are travelling very fast in a car
I politicians make mistakes

5 Listen for main ideas. You are going to hear Jean talking about things in the list. Which things does she talk about? How does she feel about them?

6 Work in groups. Think of an event which has made you feel happy, sad, frightened, worried or excited.

Make notes on:
- when and where it happened
- what you were doing at the time
- what happened
- what you did when it happened
- how you felt about it

Tell the other students in your group about the event, and react to what they tell you.

7 Write a paragraph about the event. Use your notes to help you.

8 Look at David's checklist for his trip to Sri Lanka. Say what he needs to do before he goes.

Example: He needs to buy some camera film.

1 Arrange interviews
2 Collect plane ticket
3 Buy camera film
4 Order travellers' cheques
5 Have injections
6 Start taking anti-malaria tablets
7 Pack suitcase
8 Check recording equipment
9 Book taxi to airport

9 Predict before listening. Work in pairs. David is going to Sri Lanka tomorrow. Which things on the list do you think he's already done?

10 Listen for main ideas. Which things has David already done? Compare your answers with your partner. Did you guess correctly in 9? Write sentences about what David has already done, and what he hasn't done yet.

11 Work in pairs. Think of three things you need to take on a trip to:

- the African jungle
- the French Riviera
- the Himalayas
- the Sahara Desert
- Britain

Write sentences explaining why you should take these things.

12 Make a list of the things you need to take on a trip round your country. Now work in pairs. Ask and say what you should take on the trip, and why.

54

13   Read Annie's letter of complaint. Notice the position of:

- the writer's address
- the date
- the address of the shop
- the beginning of the letter
- the end of the letter

1, Regal Crescent,
Edinburgh

17 September 1987

The Manager,
Highland Video,
14, Princes Street,
Edinburgh

Dear Sir/Madam,
    I am returning the video cassette of the film 'Cabaret', which I bought from your shop last week. When I played it, I found it was a video of a football match.
Please would you either send me a replacement or refund my money.
    Yours faithfully,
    Annie MacDonald
Annie MacDonald

Write a letter of complaint to a shop in your town about one of the items below. Use Annie's letter as a model.

- an electric kettle that blew up
- a clock that went backwards
- a thriller with the last chapter missing
- a bottle of perfume which contained lemonade

14   Role play. Work in pairs. Act out telephone dialogues about one of the items above. Change roles when you have finished.

15   Build your vocabulary. Look back over Units 7 to 11, and write five words in each of the categories below.

LEISURE ACTIVITIES   ENTERTAINMENT   FEELINGS   TRAVEL EQUIPMENT

Unit 13

Describing processes and events

**1   Predict before reading. Work in pairs.
During his trip to Sri Lanka, David Piper wants
to visit a tea plantation. You are going to read a
passage explaining how tea is produced. Before
you read, discuss what you know about tea
production. Use these verbs to help you:**

grow   pick   dry   store   sell

**2   Read and connect ideas. Put the sections of
the passage in the right order.**

A First the leaves are spread out on nylon
   shelves until they lose some of their moisture.
   Next the leaves are passed through rolling
   machines.

B The black tea is graded and stored in chests.
   Over ninety per cent of Ceylon tea is sold in
   Colombo, which is the largest tea auction
   centre in the world. Most of Sri Lanka's tea is
   exported to Britain, and smaller quantities are
   bought by countries all over the world.

C The rolled leaves are then spread out again,
   this time on tables, and they turn brown as
   they absorb oxygen. After that, the leaves are
   dried in hot air and they turn black.

D Tea is made from the dried leaves of an
   evergreen plant which is called the Chinese
   Camellia. The green leaves are usually picked

by hand, and then taken to the factory by
truck.

E Even people who have never heard of Sri
   Lanka know about Ceylon tea. And with good
   reason. More tea is produced on this small
   island than in any other country on earth,
   with the exception of India. Most of Sri
   Lanka's tea is grown on plantations in the
   beautiful green hill country.

📼 **Listen and check.**

**3   Look at grammar. Most of the verbs in the
passage are in the present simple passive.**

Tea <u>is</u>	made grown produced	The leaves <u>are</u>	picked dried spread out

**Look through the passage and find fifteen
examples of the structure.**

**Now work in pairs. Check your answers with
your partner.**
**Then work out a rule about how to form the
present simple passive.**

4 Work in pairs. Look at the map. Ask and answer questions about where the different crops are grown/produced.

Examples: – Is coffee produced in Brazil?
  – Yes, it is.

  – Are bananas grown in Spain?
  – No, they aren't.

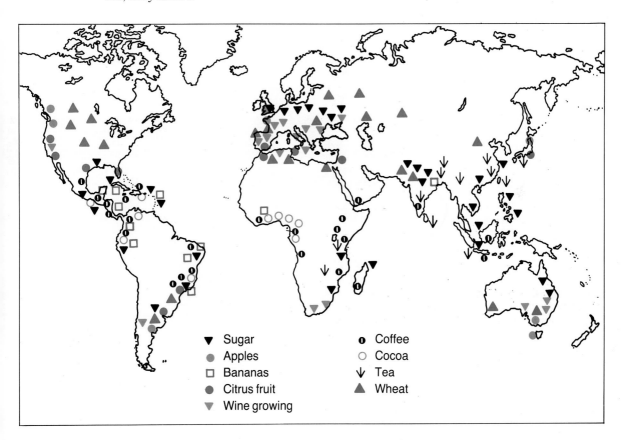

▼ Sugar	o Coffee
● Apples	○ Cocoa
□ Bananas	↓ Tea
● Citrus fruit	▲ Wheat
▼ Wine growing	

5 Build your vocabulary. Put the words below under the correct headings.

Examples:

Agricultural production	Minerals	Manufactured goods
rubber	iron	computers

iron watches tobacco computers rice
oranges rubber cotton silver oil coal
leather goods wine cars copper paper
beans diamonds gold perfume cameras

Work in pairs and check your answers. Then write two more words under each heading.

6 Work in pairs. Choose ten items from the list in 5. Then write ten sentences saying where the different items come from.

	grown	
... is/are	made produced mined manufactured	in ...

7 Decide which are your country's most important products. Then write a few sentences about your country, saying where each item is produced.

8   Read for specific information. This passage is about Buddhism. Look through the passage, and find out:

1 what Buddhism is
2 when Buddhism was founded
3 who it was founded by
4 when Buddhism was introduced into Sri Lanka

Buddhism is one of the great Oriental religions. It was founded in India in the sixth century BC by a Hindu prince, who was called the Buddha, or 'Enlightened One'. He left his palace and his wife and child because he wanted to think about the problem of human suffering. After six years of studying, he sat down under a tree (the Bo-tree), and finally he understood the reason for people's unhappiness. According to Buddha, we are unhappy because we are attached to people and things in a world where nothing is permanent. We can find peace of mind by following the right path, and through meditation. Buddha is not a god; he is a guide to truth and self-knowledge.

Buddhism was introduced into Sri Lanka over 2200 years ago by the son of an Indian Emperor, and beautiful Buddhist temples were built all over the island. Today, over two-thirds of the population of Sri Lanka are Buddhists.

Check your answers with another student.

9   Deal with difficult vocabulary. Look at these words from the passage:

palace	permanent	peace	mind
meditation	god	truth	temple

For each word:

● decide what type of word it is
● try to guess its general sense from the rest of the sentence
● discuss what you think the word means with another student.

Then check the words in your dictionary. Did you guess correctly?
Now read the passage again.

10   Look at grammar. Look at these sentences from the passage. Decide what type of word (verb or past participle) is missing.

1 It was . . . in India in the sixth century BC by a Hindu prince, who was . . . the Buddha.
2 He . . . his palace and his wife and child because he . . . to think about the problem of human suffering.
3 He . . . down under a tree, and finally he . . . the reason for people's unhappiness.
4 Buddhism was . . . into Sri Lanka over 2200 years ago, and beautiful Buddhist temples were . . . all over the island.

Now think of words to complete the sentences. Compare your answers with another student. Then look at the passage and check.

11 🔲 Listen for main ideas. You are going to hear David talking about these photographs of famous landmarks in Sri Lanka. Number the photographs in the order you hear them described.

B

A

C

12 🔲 Work in pairs.

STUDENT **A**

Listen for specific information, and find out:

1 what was built on top of Sigiriya
2 when Sigiriya was discovered again
3 what the white building is called
4 when Buddha's tooth was taken to Kandy
5 when the branch of the tree was brought to Sri Lanka

STUDENT **B**

Listen for specific information, and find out:

6 when the palace was built
7 who Sigiriya was rediscovered by
8 when Buddha's tooth was brought to Sri Lanka
9 how old the tree is
10 who the tree was brought to Sri Lanka by

13 Work in pairs. Use the information you noted down in 12 to write a short paragraph about each of the photographs in 11.

14 Work in pairs. You are going to make a visitors' guide to the town where you are now. Find out the history of a famous building or landmark in the town. Tell the rest of the class about it, with the help of notes, and a picture if possible.

Say:
- what the building/landmark is called
- where it is
- when it was built
- who it was built by
- why it is worth visiting

Then write a short paragraph. Collect all the paragraphs and pictures in a folder to make a visitors' guide to the town.

Pronunciation and Structure Review: page 145.

Unit 14 Telling a story

1 Read and connect ideas. During his tour of Scotland, Robert plans to visit Glamis Castle. Read the passage, and decide where these phrases should go.

A who died soon after gambling with the devil
B where several men and women were locked up
C which no one has been able to find
D who visits the quiet little chapel
E which stands in the Valley of Strathmore
F who hanged himself there
G who was once seen
H which open by themselves
I whose mother and sister were born there
J where King Duncan was murdered

Glamis Castle, . . . about ten miles north of Dundee, is the oldest inhabited and most striking of all the castles in Scotland. The tower was built in the fourteenth century, but most of the present building dates from the seventeenth century. The castle was well known to many kings and queens including Mary Queen of Scots and Queen Elizabeth II, ...

This magnificent castle is also famous for its mysterious legends. There's a famous secret room . . . , and there's a permanent bloodstain on the floor . . . . There are doors . . . , even though they are locked. There are stories of a family monster, a vampire, and half a dozen ghosts.

Among the ghosts, there is the terrifying apparition of the huge bearded Lord Crawford . . . . The Queen Mother's sister said that while she was living at Glamis, children often woke up screaming at night because they had seen a huge man with a beard. There is a room called the Hangman's Chamber, which is haunted by the ghost of a servant . . . , and there is the Haunted Chamber, . . . and left to die. They had come to the castle to ask for shelter. The ghost most often seen these days is the Grey Lady, ... There is also a ghost known as the White Lady, . . . by three different people at the same time. As one visitor said: 'If you stay here, any one of these ghosts may open your bedroom door.'

Check your answers with another student.

2 Read for specific information. Find out:

1 three reasons why Glamis Castle is famous
2 how many ghosts are mentioned
3 the other mysterious legends

3 Look at grammar. Complete this passage. Use: *who   whose   which   or   where*

Robert took the train from Edinburgh to Dundee, . . . is on the east coast of Scotland. He found a cheap hotel . . . he could stay the night, and then he went to a pub . . . he could get something to eat. He talked to an old lady . . . son was living in Canada. He also met a man . . . had seen a ghost at Glamis Castle.

4  Listen for specific information. Robert reacts with interest and surprise during the conversation about Glamis Castle. Which of these adjectives do you hear?

That's How	extraordinary! interesting! exciting! incredible! amazing! awful! terrible! dreadful!

Which ghost did the man see?

5 Robert also shows interest and surprise by reacting with short questions, for example: *Was it?*, *Don't you?* Write the questions he asks in reaction to these statements.

1 I don't like the place myself.
2 It's full of ghosts.
3 I've seen one.
4 I saw a ghost in Glamis Castle.
5 My wife saw it too.
6 It was a ghost.
7 It suddenly disappeared. Just like that.
8 We've never been back to the castle since.

 Listen and check.

6 Listen for main ideas. Match each news story with one of the cartoons below, and react with an appropriate comment.

7 Listen to the last news story again and try to write it down word for word. Use the outline below to help you.

A girl . . . . When . . . London flat, ... The unlucky man . . . hook. He . . . . He . . . .

Check your story with another student.

61

8 Read and connect ideas. Work in pairs, and put the sections of the story in the right order.

A The train was quite full. After he had found a seat, he took a photograph out of his jacket pocket, and studied it carefully. 'Not long to wait,' he thought.

B The girl looked doubtful. 'Doesn't he live here any more?' The girl said nothing, and then an old man with grey hair appeared behind her.
'What do you want?' he said. 'I'm Anthony Fisher.'

C He checked his jacket pocket, and then he picked up his small bag, and left the room. He paid his bill before going into the hotel dining room for breakfast.

D The young man woke up early. He had thought about this day for six months. He got up and looked out of the window.

E After paying the driver, he walked up to the front door. Suddenly, he felt very nervous.

'Calm down,' he told himself. 'It's too late to turn back now.'

F The sun was trying to shine through the mist, and the early morning traffic was beginning to thunder through the city streets. He took a shower and he got dressed quickly.

G He knocked, and the door was opened by a young girl. 'Hello,' he said. 'I'm looking for Anthony Fisher.'

H He got off at the small country station, and asked the one taxi waiting to take him to the White Farm. Fifteen minutes later, the taxi pulled up outside the old farmhouse that he had seen so many times in his dreams.

I He left the hotel and he took a bus to the station. He had a cup of coffee before he got on the train to Winterdene.

Check your story with another pair.

9 Look at grammar. Study these sentences.

He paid his bill	and (then) he went before he went before <u>going</u>	into the hotel dining room.

He paid the driver and (then) After <u>paying</u> the driver,	he walked up to the front door.

Now rewrite the sentences below. Use: *before* or *after* + *—ing*

1 He checked his jacket pocket and then he left the room.
2 He left the hotel and he took a bus to the station.
3 He had a cup of coffee before he got on the train to Winterdene.
4 He found a seat and then he studied the photograph.

10 Look at grammar. Study these sentences.

After he <u>had</u> found a seat, he studied the photograph.
After he <u>had</u> paid the driver, he walked up to the front door.

Now rewrite these sentences, Use: *after* + past perfect.

1 After taking a shower, he got dressed quickly.
2 He picked up his small bag and left the room.
3 After paying the bill, he went into the hotel dining room for breakfast.
4 He took a bus to the station and then he had a cup of coffee.

11 Predict before listening. Work in pairs and discuss these questions.

● Why do you think today is so important for the young man?
● Why does he feel nervous?
● What is special about the photograph?
● Why do you think he wants to see Anthony Fisher?

Try to guess what happens in the last part of the story.

🎚 **Now listen and check.**

12 Read and predict. Work in pairs. The passage below is the true story of an extraordinary event, but there are some missing words. Try to fill in the blanks.

. . . 6.30 p.m. . . . Christmas Eve, 1977, Thomas Helms made . . . unexpected appearance . . . national TV. . . . jumping from the 86th . . . of the Empire State Building, he . . . blown by strong . . . through an 82nd floor . . . into the NBC News studio. . . . he . . . landed in the studio, . . . he was . . . by millions of TV viewers, Thomas Helms . . . he was lucky to be . . . !

🎚 **Now listen and check.**

13 Write a short paragraph about an extraordinary event which made you feel surprised or shocked. Then tell your story to other students, and react to their stories.

Pronunciation and Structure Review: page 146.

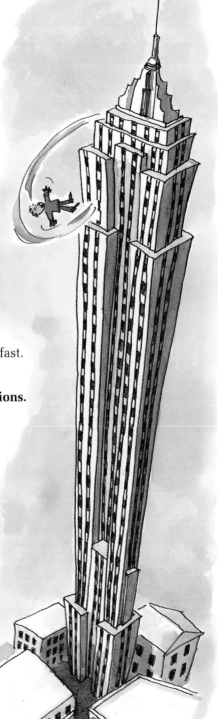

Saying what you think

1 🔲 **Listen for main ideas. Jean is giving a talk with slides about art in Barcelona. She talks about three works which are shown below. Match each work with its artist/architect. Choose from these people:**

Francesc Domingo
Antonio Gaudí
Ramon Casas
Pablo Picasso
Salvador Dalí
Joan Miró

A

B

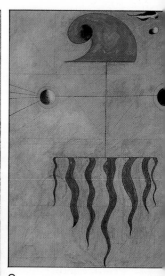

C

2 Build your vocabulary. Work in pairs and look at the adjectives below. Which adjectives would you use to describe something you like? Which adjectives would you use to describe something you don't like, or aren't sure about? Make two lists.

amusing	disgusting	amazing
ugly	colourful	beautiful
extraordinary	interesting	grotesque
exciting	shocking	fantastic
frightening	strange	original
terrible	imaginative	depressing

3 🔲 **Listen to Jean's talk again. Which of the adjectives in 2 do you hear?**

4 Work in pairs. Which adjectives would you use to describe the pictures? Does your partner agree with you?

Example: — I think this painting is rather shocking.
— Yes, but it's very imaginative.

Agreeing	*Disagreeing*
Yes, I think so too.	Well, I'm not sure.
I don't think so either.	I don't think so.
So do I./Nor do I.	I disagree/don't agree.
I (quite) agree.	Yes, but . . .

5 Write a short description of a painting or building which you think is interesting, and say why you like or don't like it.
Now tell other students about it.

6  Listen for specific
information. Jean is telling Bill
about what happened during
an excursion to Sitges, a pretty
seaside town near Barcelona.
Listen and match the names of
the tourists with the problems.

Mr Phillips
Miss Imbert
Mr Adams
Mrs Birch
Mr and Mrs Sinclair

. . . got lost.
. . . complained all the time.
. . . nearly drowned.
. . . got badly sunburnt.
. . . felt very ill.

7 Look at the phrases below, and use them to criticise the tourists in 6. Say one thing each of the
people should have done, and one thing they shouldn't have done.

Examples: Mr Phillips should have worn a life jacket.
He shouldn't have gone sailing on his own.

He She They	should shouldn't	have . . .

A wear a life jacket
B stay on the beach for so long
C come to Spain
D leave the group
E drink less wine

F go sailing on his own
G look at a map
H stay at home
I wear a hat
J eat so much

Now listen and check.

8 Write sentences criticising the tourists. Begin each sentence with *Why did . . . ?* or with *Why
didn't . . . ?*

Examples: Why didn't Mr Phillips wear a life jacket?
Why did he go sailing on his own?

9 Role play. Work in pairs.

> **STUDENT A**
>
> You are one of the tourists in 6.
>
> **Tell Student B what went wrong during your
> excursion to Sitges.**

> **STUDENT B**
>
> You are Jean.
>
> **Listen to Student A and say what he/she
> should and shouldn't have done.**

> You should(n't) have . . .
> Why did(n't) you . . . ?

Change roles and partners when you have finished.

10 Work in pairs. Think about a trip or holiday where you had problems. Tell your partner what
went wrong and why. Discuss what you should and shouldn't have done.

11 Build your vocabulary. Match the words below with the numbered items in Picture A.

typewriter
filing cabinet
desk
chair
table
pen
address book
note pad
telephone
armchair
waste-paper bin
ash tray
photograph
clock
drawer

Check your answers with another student.

A

12 Work in pairs.
Tom was called away from his office for half an hour. Picture A shows how the room was when he left it.
Look at Picture A carefully for one minute. Try to remember where everything is.
Then cover Picture A.

When Tom came back to his office, he noticed that several things were wrong. Then he realised what was missing. Look carefully at Picture B. How many differences can you see? Say what was wrong when Tom came back to his office.

Example:

– When Tom came back, the book was on the armchair. It should have been on the desk.
– No, it shouldn't! It should have been on the table.

What was missing when Tom returned?

B

13 Work in pairs and discuss the situations below. Say what you think each person should have done, and why. Use the expressions for agreeing and disagreeing in 4.

I think I don't think	he/she/they should have . . . , because . . .

1 Paul found a five pound note in the street. There was no one in sight, so he picked it up and decided to keep it. Do you think he was right?

2 Sally and Maria were very good friends. Sally knew that Maria's boyfriend was also going out with Kate. Maria didn't know about this, and Sally didn't tell her. Do you think Sally was right?

3 Ben's aunt gave him a pullover for his birthday. Ben told his aunt that he would never wear the pullover because he didn't like the colour. His aunt was quite upset. What do you think Ben should have done?

4 Tom and Jill had dinner in an expensive restaurant. The food wasn't very good, and the service was slow. When the bill arrived, the waiter had forgotten to charge them for a bottle of wine they had drunk. They paid the bill without saying anything about the mistake. Do you think they were right?

5 Richard is a policeman. His sister, Margaret, has three young children and very little money. Richard discovered that Margaret sometimes stole food from the supermarket where she worked, so he reported her to the supermarket manager. Do you think he was right?

6 A car was driving along a motorway when a suitcase on the roof rack fell off in the middle of the road. The driver immediately stopped the car at the side of the motorway, and ran back to pick up the case. Was the driver right?

14 [cassette] Listen to two people discussing the situations in 13. What do they think each person should have done? Do you agree with them?

15 Choose three of the situations in 13, and write a couple of sentences saying what you think about each one.

Example: I don't think Richard should have reported Margaret to the supermarket manager, because he's her brother. He should have told her not to steal food.

Pronunciation and Structure Review: page 148.

Persuading people to do things

1 Predict before listening. Sriyani, a tourist guide, gives David some advice about travelling in the Sri Lanka hill country. Match the advice with the reasons.

Advice

1 Drive carefully.
2 Leave early.
3 Pack some warm clothes.
4 Take an umbrella.
5 Take plenty of camera film.

Reasons

A It's the rainy season.
B The roads aren't very good.
C The hill country is very beautiful.
D It gets cold at night.
E You have to drive slowly.

▣▣ **Listen and check.**

2 Write five sentences saying what Sriyani tells David to do and why.

Example: She tells him to drive carefully, because . . .

3 Complete the dialogue with Sriyani's advice. Use the phrases in 1 and the expressions below.

> You'd better . . .
> If I were you, I'd . . .
> You should . . .
> You ought to . . .

DAVID:	We're driving to the hill country at the weekend.
SRIYANI:	. . . .
DAVID:	Oh dear. I hope we don't have an accident.
SRIYANI:	. . . .
DAVID:	That's a good idea.
SRIYANI:	. . . .
DAVID:	Really? Then I'll take a couple of pullovers.
SRIYANI:	. . . .
DAVID:	What? Do you think it's going to rain?
SRIYANI:	. . . .
DAVID:	I suppose you're right.
SRIYANI:	. . . .
DAVID:	Yes, I want to take lots of photos. Thanks for the advice.

Now work in pairs and act out the dialogue.

4 Role play. Work in pairs.

> **STUDENT A**
>
> **Choose one of the situations below and ask Student B for advice.**
>
> - You can't sleep at night.
> - You want to buy a present for a friend.
> - You've lost the keys to your flat.
> - You often forget things.
> - You are worried about an exam.
> - You want to be famous.

> **STUDENT B**
>
> **Listen to Student A's problem, and give some sensible advice, and a warning.**

> You'd better (not) . . .
> If I were you, I would(n't) . . .
> You should(n't) . . .
> You ought(n't) to . . .

Now change roles and partners, and choose another situation.

5 Look at these statements about customs. Say if they are true or false for your country.

A You must shake hands when you meet someone.

B You must shake your head for yes.

C You can take photographs anywhere without a permit.

D You must ask people first before taking a photograph of them.

E You mustn't wear shoes in a church or temple.

F You have to cover your head in a church or temple.

G You can eat with your fingers.

H You can't eat with your left hand.

> You must . . .   You have to . . .
> You don't have to . . .   You don't need to . . .
> You mustn't . . .   You can't . . .   You aren't allowed to . . .
> You can . . .

6 📼 **Listen for main ideas. David wants to know about customs in Sri Lanka. Listen to the conversation, and decide if the statements in 5 are true or false.**
Now work in pairs. Check your answers by telling your partner about the customs in Sri Lanka.

7 📼 **Listen for main ideas. Listen to a conversation about British customs, and decide if the statements in 5 are true or false for Britain.**

8 Look at the list in 5 again. What did Sriyani tell David to do? What did she tell him not to do?

Examples: She told him to ask people before taking a photograph of them.
She told him not to shake hands.

9 Write a simple instruction on a piece of paper, for example: CLOSE YOUR EYES. Give the piece of paper to the student on your right. He/She must carry out the instruction. The other students in the class must guess exactly what you told the student to do.

Example: – Did you tell her to go to sleep?
– No, I didn't.

– You told her to close her eyes.
– That's right!

10 Read for main ideas. These sentences are from _On the Road in Great Britain_. Match the sentences with the paragraph headings.

DRIVING ON THE LEFT   ACCIDENTS

MOTORWAYS   SEAT BELTS   PARKING

A You are not allowed to make U-turns or to reverse.

B Drivers and front-seat passengers must wear them when travelling in Britain.

C In general you must not park within ten metres of a junction.

D People using the roads drive on the left and overtake on the right.

E You must inform the police immediately.

F The driver must make sure that they are properly fastened.

G It is also illegal and dangerous to leave your car at a pedestrian crossing.

H You must not stop just to have a rest; if you wish to stop, you should continue until the next exit or service station.

I If you are driving at night, remember that headlights must be dipped to the left.

J The emergency number for this (and for the fire and ambulance service) is 999.

K Other no-parking areas are usually marked by road signs or by yellow lines on the edge of roads.

L Learner drivers, pedestrians, moped riders and cyclists are not allowed to use them.

M If you are walking, remember to look to the right when starting to cross a road.

11 Build your vocabulary. Look at the sentences in 10 and find:

- five verbs connected with driving
- six nouns referring to people
- three emergency services
- eight more nouns connected with the rules of the road

You can use your dictionary.
Check your answers with another student.

12 Work in pairs. Look at the rules of the road, and find:

- four things you must do when driving in Britain
- three things you mustn't do when driving on motorways
- something pedestrians can't do
- something pedestrians should do
- two places where you aren't allowed to park

Now write sentences about these rules.

Example: In Britain, you must drive on the left and you must overtake on the right.

13 Compare the rules of the road in Britain with the rules of the road in your country. What are the differences?

Example: In Britain, drivers have to wear seatbelts, but they don't have to in my country.

14  Listen for specific information. Three people are asking for permission to do something. Which phrases do you hear?

Asking for permission

Do you mind if I . . . ?
May I . . . ?
Can I . . . ?
Could I . . . ?

Giving permission

Not at all – go ahead.
Yes, you can.
Yes, of course.
Oh, all right then.

Refusing permission

I'd rather you didn't.
No, I'm afraid you can't.
I'm sorry, but you aren't allowed to.

15 Role play.
Work in pairs. Choose one of these situations and act it out using the phrases in 14.

A and **B** are friends:
- **A** wants to borrow one of **B**'s favourite records.
- **A** wants to watch a programme on television at **B**'s house.
- **A** wants to make a phone call at **B**'s house.

A is a student; **B** is a teacher:
- **A** wants to leave the class early.
- **A** wants to borrow one of the class cassettes for the evening.
- **A** wants to smoke in the classroom.

Now change roles and partners, and choose another situation.

Pronunciation and Structure Review: page 150.

Unit 17 Speculating

THE HIGHLANDS

John O'Groa[...]

Inverness
Carrbridge
Aviemore
Kingussie
Newtonmore
Dalwhinnie
Blair Atholl
Fort William
Pitlochry
Dunkeld
Dundee
Perth
Oban
Aber[...]
Loch Long
Helensburgh
Glasgow
Edinburgh

1 🔲 **Listen and infer. Robert is still touring Scotland. Listen to the conversation, and look at the timetable. Find out:**

- which station Robert is at
- what time it is

Discuss the answers with your partner.

Monday to Saturday

Perth	01 10	04 57	05 55	08 50	10 50	13 50	14 50	18 20	
Dunkeld	01 34	05 17	06 19	09 07	11 08	14 08			
Pitlochry	01 51	05 36	06 35	09 23	11 24	14 24	15 26	18 54	
Blair Atholl	02 05	05 50	06 47	09 36	11 35	14 38			
Dalwhinnie			07 28		12 08	15 06			
Newtonmore	03 02	06 37	07 40	10 13	12 20	15 18			
Kingussie	03 10	06 42	07 46	10 18	12 32	15 23	16 16	19 47	
Aviemore	03 47	06 58	08 01	10 32	12 46	15 43	16 30	20 00	
Carrbridge		07 09	08 17	10 40	12 55	15 52			
Inverness	04 50	07 55	09 20	11 22	13 35	16 35	17 19	20 42	

2 Look at grammar. Make indirect questions.

Example:

Which platform does the Inverness train leave from?
Do you know . . . ?
Do you know which platform the Inverness train leaves from?

1 When does the next train leave?   Can you tell me . . . ?
2 What time does it arrive?   Do you know . . . ?
3 What am I going to do?   I don't know . . . .
4 Is there a cheap hotel near the station?   I wonder . . . .
5 How much does it cost?   Have you any idea . . . ?
6 What should I do?   I wonder . . .

🔲 **Listen again and check.**

3 Say what Robert wants to know.

Example: He wants to know where the Inverness train leaves from.

4 Act out the dialogue between Robert and the porter.

5 Work in groups. Discuss what you would do if you were Robert, and explain why.

I'd	wait for the next train to Inverness look for a hotel sleep in my tent go back to Pitlochry	because . . .

6 Role play. Work in pairs. Use the timetable in 1 to answer your partner's questions.

> **STUDENT A**
> It is 9 a.m. You are in Aviemore, and you want to get the next train to Inverness.
>
> **Ask Student B when the train leaves, and how long it takes.**

> **STUDENT B**
> It is midday and you are in Perth. You want to get to Newtonmore as soon as possible.
>
> **Ask Student A when the next train leaves, and what time it arrives.**

Can you tell me I want to know I'd like to know	when what time . . . ? how long

7 Look at this photograph.

Have you any idea what it is?
Where do you think it was taken?

I wonder what it is. I wonder if it . . . Perhaps it . . . Maybe it . . . I think it . . .

8 📼 Listen for specific information. Work in pairs.

> **STUDENT A**
>
> **Listen and note down the answers to these questions:**
>
> 1 How far is Loch Ness from Inverness?
> 2 What is the Loch Ness Monster supposed to look like?
> 3 How wide is Loch Ness?
> 4 How deep is it?

> **STUDENT B**
>
> **Listen and note down the answers to these questions:**
>
> 5 Is Loch Ness the deepest lake in England?
> 6 When was the photo taken?
> 7 How long is Loch Ness?
> 8 What colour is the water?

9 Work in pairs. Find out the answers to your partner's questions.

Examples: Can you tell me how far Loch Ness is from Inverness?
Do you know if it's the deepest lake in England?

10 Work in groups. Do you think there is something in Loch Ness? If so, what?

I wonder if . . . Perhaps . . . There may be . . .	I (don't) think . . . I'm sure . . . There's definitely (not) . . .

73

11 Look carefully at the photographs. What are these objects?
Discuss your ideas with another student.

Examples: – Have you any idea what A is?
– I'm not sure, but I think it must be part of a . . .
– It looks like a . . .
– Perhaps it's a . . .

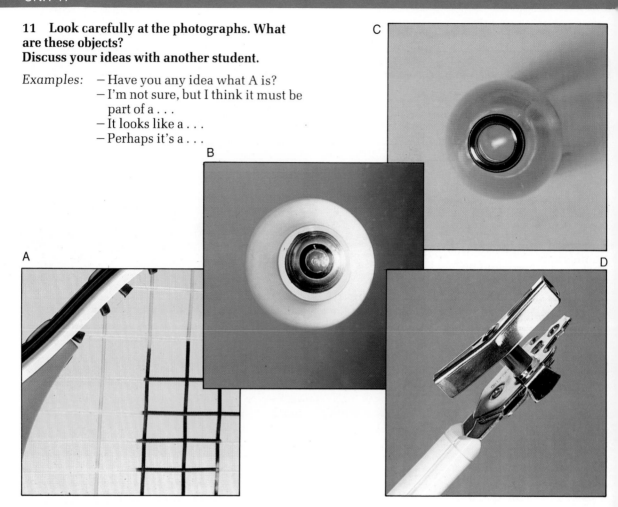

12 Work in pairs. Arthur, Barbara, Carol, Donald and Ella are five brothers and sisters.
They all live in different countries: Brazil, Canada, France, Japan and Sweden.
They all have different occupations: businessman, doctor, journalist, teacher and spy.
Discuss the clues, and work out who lives where, and what each person's occupation is.

CLUES
Barbara is not a doctor.
Carol lives in South America.
One of the brothers is a teacher.
The journalist lives in France.
The businessman lives in Japan.
Donald lives in Canada.

Examples: Carol lives in South America, so she <u>must</u> live in . . .
Donald lives in Canada, so he <u>can't</u> be the businessman.

	OCCUPATION	COUNTRY
ARTHUR		
BARBARA		
CAROL		
DONALD		
ELLA		

13 Listen for main ideas. What do you think the people are talking about? Listen again, and write down the words that give you clues. Then discuss your conclusions with other students. Do you agree?

14 Read for main ideas. This passage was written by Paul Theroux. He describes a travelling companion on the train from Glasgow to Oban. Read through the passage and find out:

- what Mr Davidson was carrying
- why he was carrying them

'I'm going to Oban,' I said.

'Good,' he said. 'We can talk.' He was also going the hundred miles.

But he did most of the talking. He was very old and even sitting next to me he was a foot higher. He looked like a pope. He had a fat nose and big baggy-fleshed hands. He wore a long black overcoat and carried a small parcel of books tied with twine: detective stories. His name was John L. Davidson, and he had been born in Lanarkshire in 1895.

He said, 'I'm only seven years younger than John Logie Baird. Have you not heard of him? He invented the tellyvision. He was born here in Helensburgh.'

We came to Garelochhead, we travelled past Loch Long. The mountains above it were dark and rough, like enormous pieces of dusty coal. They were surrounded by pinewoods. The loch was blue-black and looked depthless.

'This loch is so long, so deep and so straight they test torpedoes in it,' Mr Davidson said. 'You can shoot a torpedo from one end to the other – thirteen miles or more. Want to see something interesting?'

He stood up and beckoned me to the window, and slid it down and said 'Watch.'

We were coming to a junction, more tracks, and an isolated signal box. There were woods and hills all around. I expected the train to stop, but it did not even slow down. Mr Davidson stuck his parcel of books out of the window and dangled it. A railwayman was standing on a small raised platform near the signal box. He snatched the books and yelled, 'Thank you!'

'I've come this way before. The trains don't stop. I heard that the signalman here likes to read a good book. There's no shop here, no library, so I brought those books for him.'

Mr Davidson had no idea who the signalman was, nor did he know his name. He only knew that the signalman liked to read a good book.

15 Deal with difficult vocabulary. Read the passage again, and write down any words that you do not understand. Look at each word.

- What type of word is it?
- Can you guess the general sense from the rest of the sentence?

Try to work out the meaning of *five* words in this way. Then discuss your ideas with another student.

I'm not sure what . . . means. Have you any idea what . . . means?	I think it must mean . . . Perhaps it means . . .

Finally, check the words in your dictionary. Did you guess correctly? Now read the passage again.

16 Work in groups. Discuss these questions.

1 How far is it from Glasgow to Oban?
2 Why did Mr Davidson look 'like a pope'?
3 When was John Logie Baird born?

4 Why do you think television is spelt 'tellyvision'?
5 Did Mr Davidson know the signalman?

Pronunciation and Structure Review: page 152.

Checking what you know

1 Predict before reading. Work in pairs. In the passage below, a Spanish olive grower explains how olive oil is produced. Before you read, decide which of the following words you expect to find in the passage.

tree	hospital	price	black
sugar	red	plantation	ripe
green	visa	factory	pick
guitar	finally	comfortable	phone
introduce	letter	travel	farmer

2 Look at grammar. Read the passage, and put the verbs in brackets into the present passive.

Example: (grow) → are grown

Olive oil is one of Spain's most important products. Olives (grow) all along the Mediterranean coast, from Catalunya down to Andalucia. My family has owned a plantation of about 600 trees for many generations. The olive tree grows to a very great age – normally it is over 100 years old.

Olives (use) mainly for making olive oil, although some (sell) for eating. You may have eaten both green and black olives. The only difference between them is that the green ones (pick) in September when the olive is unripe; the black ones (pick) a couple of months later, when the olive is fully ripe. Black olives (use) to make oil.

When olives (pick), two large sheets of plastic (place) under the tree on each side of the trunk, so that all the olives will fall on the plastic. Then the olives (pull) off the branches with a sort of wooden hand on the end of a long wooden pole – which is what I do – or the branches (knock) with a pole until the olives fall to the ground. Then the olives (take) to the factory where they (clean). After that, they (crush) into a paste and finally the oil (extract).

The price farmers get for olive oil (fix) by the government, and it is very low. For one of my olive trees, I get about 5 kilos of oil and I get 100 to 150 pesetas a kilo, depending on the quality. So I get about 750 pesetas from each tree.

3 Write a short paragraph about one of the most important products from your country.

Say: • where it is grown/made/produced
  • how it is produced: First . . .
   Next . . .
   Then . . .
   After that, . . .
   Finally . . .

Use the passage in 2 and the description of tea production in Unit 13 to help you.

4  Listen for specific information. Work in pairs. Robert is talking to a travelling companion on the coach from Inverness to Oban. Listen to Robert talking about his life.

STUDENT A

Find out:

1 where he was born
2 where he lived in Canada first
3 when he went to university
4 how long he stayed at university
5 how long he worked in a theatre
6 when he started work as a salesman

STUDENT B

Find out:

7 when he went to Canada
8 when he moved to Toronto
9 where he went to university
10 when he left university
11 when he applied for a job as a salesman
12 how long he has had the job

5 Work in pairs. Ask and answer questions to find out about other important events in Robert's life. Then complete these sentences with *before* or *after*.

1 . . . living in Edinburgh for ten years, Robert went to Canada.
2 He lived in Winnipeg . . . moving to Montreal.
3 He went to university . . . leaving school.
4 He worked in a theatre . . . going to university.
5 . . . starting work as a salesman, he worked in a theatre.

6 Look at grammar. Write five sentences about Robert's life using *after* + past perfect.

Example: Robert went to Canada after he <u>had</u> <u>lived</u> in Edinburgh for ten years.

7 Work in groups. Each member of the group should find out a few facts about the life of a famous person. Tell the rest of your group about the person. Do not say who it is! The group must try to guess who the person is.

Example: He was born in 1881 in Malaga, Spain. He went to the art academy in Barcelona before studying in Madrid. After settling in Paris in 1904, he became famous for his Cubist paintings. He died in 1973.

> Perhaps it's . . .
> It can't be . . .
> It must be . . .

8 Read for main ideas. The passage on the right gives advice and warnings for travellers abroad. Which three things do you think are the most important? Does your partner agree with you?

9 This tourist has just arrived at his holiday resort. He is looking for a restaurant for lunch. What advice would you give him? Use the list in 8.

Examples: If I were you, I wouldn't wear that hat.
You'd better not eat too much.

Travelling without tears

Travelling abroad is exciting, but things can go wr
Unfortunately, street crime is on the increase in n
countries, particularly in big cities and tourist resorts. B
you take a few sensible precautions, you should hav
carefree trip.

- Take out insurance against illness, accident, and
before you go.
- Keep details of your travellers' cheques and credit ca
so you can report their loss.
- If you are driving, check local traffic regulations
advance.
- Don't take expensive jewellery or watches.
- Carry your passport in a safe place.
- Keep your camera hidden in a bag (*not* an airline trav
bag).
- Don't carry large amounts of cash with you.
- Keep your money in your pocket, not in a handbag.
- Check exchange rates before changing money.
- Check the dates of public holidays (when shops and
banks are closed).
- If you must take valuables, leave them in the hotel safe.
- If you leave things in your car, lock them in the boot.
- Try not to look at your tourist map in public places.
- Never wear shorts or baseball caps.
- Don't eat too much for the first couple of days.
- Learn a few simple expressions in the foreign language.

Excuse me. Do you speak English?

MAP

10 The tourist is now very depressed and he feels sick. While he was having a large lunch, his passport, watch and camera were stolen and his car was broken into. He has no insurance, and he has lost the details of his travellers' cheques and credit card. He does not speak a word of the local language, so he cannot even ask where the police station is.

What would you say to him now?

Examples: I told you not to wear that hat!
You shouldn't have eaten so much.
Why didn't you hide your camera?

Now write six sentences criticising the tourist.

He should have . . .	He shouldn't have . . .

11   Build your vocabulary. Complete the sentences. Choose from the instructions on the right.

If you don't know	where a place is how to spell a word when a train leaves what's on television how to use a machine how to pronounce a word how to cook something what the date is what someone's phone number is what a word means	. . . you look at a(n)	calendar. recipe. timetable. map. instruction manual. newspaper.
		. . . you look it up in a	dictionary. telephone directory.

12   Work in pairs. Ask and answer questions about sources of information.

Example: – What do you do when you don't know when a train leaves?
            – You look at a timetable.

13   Work in groups and discuss the answers to these questions. Then compare your answers with the rest of the class.

Examples: –I wonder where Mali is.
             –I'm not sure where it is.

             –It's in Asia, isn't it?
             –I think it must be in . . .

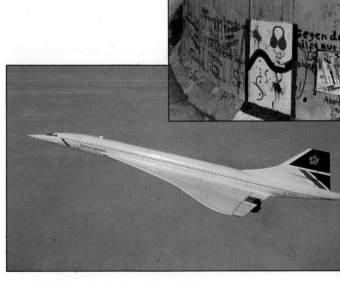

1 Where is Mali?
   a) Asia   b) Africa   c) South America
2 What's the capital of Trinidad?
   a) Kingston   b) Bridgetown   c) Port of
   Spain
3 How long does it take to fly from London to
   New York by Concorde?
   a) three hours   b) four hours   c) five hours
4 When was Martin Luther King shot?
   a) 1963   b) 1957   c) 1968
5 Who was *Fidelio* composed by?
   a) Brahms   b) Beethoven   c) Bach
6 When did the Wright brothers make their
   first flight?
   a) 1901   b) 1903   c) 1905
7 How many kilometres are there in ten miles?
   a) fourteen   b) fifteen   c) sixteen
8 What does 'illegal' mean?
   a) against the law   b) sick   c) dangerous
9 Who was *Candide* written by?
   a) Rousseau   b) Sartre   c) Voltaire
10 When was the Berlin Wall built?
   a) 1945   b) 1956   c) 1961
11 Which is the largest planet?
   a) Saturn   b) Jupiter   c) Uranus
12 Who was *Guernica* painted by?
   a) Dalí   b) Picasso   c) Miró

14   Build your vocabulary. Look back over Units 13 to 17, and write five words in each of the categories below.

CROPS   RELIGION   OFFICE EQUIPMENT   RULES OF THE ROAD   TRAIN TRAVEL

Describing things

1   Build your vocabulary. Look at the photograph. Which of the following items can you see? Use your dictionary if necessary.

soap	plate	saucepan
tin opener	washing-up liquid	frying pan
kettle	spoon	glass
knife	bottle opener	soap powder
cup	fork	bowl
corkscrew	scissors	saucer

2   Work in pairs. Ask and say what the items in 1 are for. Use the table below to help you.

Example: — What's a kettle for?
— It's for boiling water in.

It's for They're for	eating drinking cooking cutting boiling water opening tins opening bottles washing washing clothes washing up	with. out of. in. off.

Now write ten sentences.

Example: A kettle is for boiling water in.

3 📼 **Listen for specific information. Jean needs some of the items in 1. Close your books while you listen to the conversation once. Then try to remember all the things Jean needs, and write them down. Check your list with another student.**

Listen again, and check.

4   Work in pairs. Look at the items in 1, and ask and say what Jean needs.

Examples: — Does she need a kettle?
— Yes, she does.

— Does she need any cups and saucers?
— No, she doesn't.

Now write sentences saying what Jean needs.

Example: She needs a kettle.
She needs some scissors.

Labels on image: I salt · M ham · Q water · J eggs · G olive oil · F pepper · L cayenne pepper · A parsley · C celery · O cucumber · P white wine · E tomatoes · K vinegar · N potatoes · H garlic · D onions · B olives

5 Listen for specific information. Which of the ingredients is Bill going to buy?

6 Now look at the recipe ingredients below, and check. Which dish is Bill going to make?

Gazpacho	Catalan soup
½ kilo tomatoes	3 onions
¼ cucumber	50 g chopped ham
1 small onion	100 ml white wine
garlic	1 stick celery
a dozen black olives	3 tomatoes 3 potatoes
50 ml olive oil	1½ litres water
10 ml vinegar	parsley, pepper
250 ml water	
salt, pepper	Tortilla español
cayenne pepper, parsley	1 onion 2 potatoes
	4 eggs olive oil
	salt, pepper

7 Build your vocabulary. Look at the pictures, and ask and say how much or how many.

How much . . . is there?	A little./A lot.
How many . . . are there?	A few./A lot.

8 Build your vocabulary. Note down the basic ingredients for a dish you like. Then tell your partner what it's made with.

9 Work in pairs. Look at the objects and write down as many adjectives as you can to describe each one.

10 📼 Listen for specific information. Number the items in the order you hear them described.

11 Read for detail. Read the descriptions below and check your answers to 10. There is an adjective missing from each description. Can you remember the missing adjectives?

1 It's a small red one, with a white face.
2 I like the blue checked one, with short sleeves.
3 Well, it's a rectangular black leather one, with a shoulder strap.
4 It's a grey woollen one, with a big collar.
5 It's an oval gold one, with a black leather strap.
6 It's the heavy dark blue one, with a red label on it.

📼 Listen and check.

12 Put the adjectives which describe the items in 9 in the correct column in the chart. Add three more adjectives to each column.

ORDER OF ADJECTIVES						
Size/weight	Shape	Colour	Material	Where it's from	Noun	Other details
small	*square*	*red*			*clock*	*with a white face*

(rows numbered 1–6)

13 Write a short description of three of the items in 1. Pay particular attention to adjective order. Can your partner identify the items from your description?

14 Role play. Work in groups of three. Imagine you have lost something and you are telephoning the place where you think you left it. Decide what you have lost and ask to speak to someone who can help you. Answer his/her questions about it.

What	size shape colour	is it?	How	big heavy long	is it?	Where's it from? What's it made of? What's it for?

Use the telephone phrases in Unit 11 to help you.

15 🔲 Listen for detail. Look carefully at the paintings, and listen to the description. Which painting is described?

16 Read and predict. Read the description, look at the painting, and decide where the phrases below should go. Then write out the complete description.

This painting shows two people . . . .   On the right, ...   He's wearing a brown suit, ...   He's looking . . . .   Opposite him, on the left, ...   She's wearing a large hat . . . .   The waiter is standing . . . .   He's wearing a black suit, a white shirt and a black bow tie, ...   The table is small and round, ...   In the middle of the table, between the young couple, . . . and there's a small plate and a knife . . . .   Next to him, in the bottom right-hand corner of the painting, ...   In the bottom left-hand corner, ...   Behind her, ...   Behind the waiter, in the top right-hand corner, ...

Breakfast   Paul Signac

Bank Holiday   William Strang

• and covered with a white cloth • there's a bunch of yellow flowers on a chair • and long white gloves • there's a vase of orange flowers • sitting at a table in a restaurant • there's a small black dog on a chair next to the woman • in front of the man • behind the man • there's a young man • there's an elderly man • a white shirt with a black bow tie, and a brown hat • there's a cupboard with bottles on the shelves • at the menu • and he's holding a cloth under his arm • there's a young woman in a light-coloured dress with a black belt

🔲 Now listen and check.

17 Write a description of the other painting. Use the description in 16 to help you.

Pronunciation and Structure Review: page 153.

Making comparisons

1 Build your vocabulary. Which of these words are forms of transport?

airport	plane
bicycle	public
boat	ship
bus	station
car	taxi
coach	ticket
customs	timetable
garage	train
motorbike	mini-bus
petrol	visa

Check your list with your partner.

2 Predict before listening. You are going to hear a conversation about transport in Sri Lanka. Which words in 1 do you expect to hear?

🔊 Listen to David talking to an English teacher who lives in Sri Lanka, and check.

3 🔊 Listen for specific information. Listen again and decide whether the following statements are true or false.

1 It's usually more expensive to hire a chauffeur-driven car than a self-drive car.
2 The cheapest form of transport in Sri Lanka is the CTB bus.
3 Private mini-buses are much slower than CTB buses.
4 CTB buses aren't as comfortable as mini-buses.
5 The train is more expensive than the bus.
6 It's more dangerous to take the train than to drive.

Check your answers with your partner.

4 Complete these sentences to make true statements about transport in Sri Lanka.

1 It's usually . . . expensive to hire a chauffeur-driven car . . . a self-drive car.
2 The least . . . form of transport in Sri Lanka is the CTB bus.
3 Private mini-buses . . . faster . . . CTB buses.
4 Private mini-buses . . . comfortable . . . CTB buses.
5 The train isn't . . . cheap . . . the bus.
6 It's . . . dangerous to take the train . . . to drive.

🔊 **Listen again and check.**

5 Work in pairs. Read for specific information. Then make comparisons between the cost of the different types of transport.

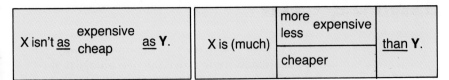

X isn't as	expensive / cheap	as Y.

X is (much)	more / less	expensive	than Y.
	cheaper		

X is the	most / least	expensive	form of transport.
	cheapest		

6 Work in groups. Look at the forms of transport you found in 1. In your experience, which form of transport is the:

- safest?
- most comfortable?
- least tiring?
- most exciting?
- cheapest?
- most interesting?
- fastest?

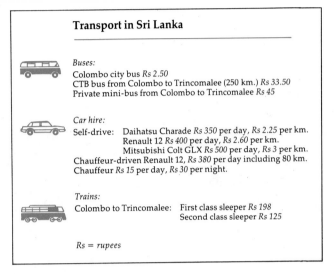

Transport in Sri Lanka

Buses:
Colombo city bus *Rs 2.50*
CTB bus from Colombo to Trincomalee (250 km.) *Rs 33.50*
Private mini-bus from Colombo to Trincomalee *Rs 45*

Car hire:
Self-drive: Daihatsu Charade *Rs 350 per day, Rs 2.25 per km.*
Renault 12 *Rs 400 per day, Rs 2.60 per km.*
Mitsubishi Colt GLX *Rs 500 per day, Rs 3 per km.*
Chauffeur-driven Renault 12, *Rs 380 per day including 80 km.*
Chauffeur *Rs 15 per day, Rs 30 per night.*

Trains:
Colombo to Trincomalee: First class sleeper *Rs 198*
Second class sleeper *Rs 125*

Rs = rupees

7 Work in pairs. What is the best way to travel:

- to the railway station from your school?
- to the nearest airport from your home?
- home from your school?
- to the other side of your country?
- to Australia from your country?

Say why.

The best way is to . . .		
go by	bicycle.	cycle.
	air, plane.	fly.
	boat, ship, sea.	sail.
	car.	drive.
	train, bus, coach, motorbike.	
go on	foot.	walk.

8 Write a short paragraph comparing *two* forms of transport, and say which you prefer.

Example: I'd rather travel by train than by plane. The plane is faster than the train, but it isn't as interesting. The train is less tiring and much cheaper. I also think the train is more comfortable than the plane, and I'm sure it's safer.

9 Predict before listening. You are going to hear a radio interview about what an average British household spends its money on. Which *twelve* of these words do you expect to hear?

transport   supermarket   interview
factory   footwear   entertainment
housing   heating   education
food   village   weather
passenger   light   household goods
alcohol   airport   midday
tobacco   park   clothing

10 📼 Listen for specific information. Listen and check your answers. Then make a list of the twelve words in the order that you heard them.

11 📼 Listen for specific information. Listen again and write down the percentage of the budget spent beside each item on your list.

Example: Transport 17%

Check your answers with another student.

12 Work in pairs. Compare the amounts spent by the British on the different items in the budget.

> They spend more/less on . . . than (they do) on . . .
> They spend (about) the same on . . . as (they do) on . . .

13 Work out approximately how much you spend on different things, and write out your own budget.
Then work in pairs and talk about your budgets.

Examples: – I spend more on clothes than (I do) on entertainment.
   – What do you spend the most on?
   – Food!

Now write sentences comparing the amounts you spend on different things.

14 Work in pairs. The clock shows how the average British family spends a working day. Ask and say what time people in Britain:

- get up
- start work/school
- have lunch
- finish work/school
- have dinner
- go to bed/sleep

15 Work in pairs. Ask and say how much time the British spend:

- having breakfast and travelling
- working
- at school
- having lunch
- doing homework
- having dinner
- watching TV or reading
- sleeping/asleep
- eating

Example:

– How much time do the British spend having lunch?
– One hour.

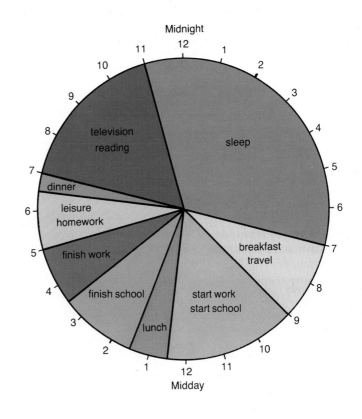

16 Work in pairs. Ask and say what time you do these things. Then work out how long your partner spends doing the things in 15.

Now compare the time you each spend doing these things.

Examples: – You spend an hour doing your homework, whereas I spend thirty minutes.
– So you spend less time doing your homework than I do.

– I spend forty-five minutes travelling, but you only spend ten minutes travelling.
– So you spend longer travelling than I do.

17 Think about the average working day for people in your country, and compare it with the average British working day.

Example: British children start school later than we do.
They start at nine o'clock, but/whereas we start at half past eight.

18 Write a paragraph describing a typical working day in your country.

Pronunciation and Structure Review: page 155.

Unit 21

Explaining how things work

1 Predict before listening. Robert is back in Annie's flat. He doesn't know how the coffee machine works. Which of these verbs do you expect to hear in Annie's instructions?

turn on	drive	plug in	pay	heat up	close
agree	inform	pour	put	press	wear
go on	open	place	fill	get on	leave

Check your answers with another student.

2 🔲 **Listen for main ideas.** As you listen to Annie's instructions, number the photographs in the right order.

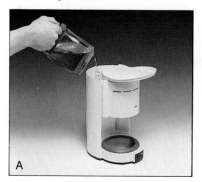

A

B

C

D

E

F

Which verbs did you hear? Listen again and check.

3 Build your vocabulary. Complete the instructions with verbs from the list in 1. (Two verbs should be used twice.)

First of all, . . . the machine and . . . the electricity. Then . . . the filter holder and . . . a filter paper inside. . . . a teaspoon of coffee per cup in the filter paper and . . . the filter holder. . . . the coffee pot with water and . . . it into the top of the machine. When you've . . . the pot under the filter again, . . . the switch at the bottom. As soon as the red light . . . , the water starts to . . . . After about five minutes, as soon as the bubbling noise stops, . . . the coffee or . . . it on the hotplate until you're ready.

4 Answer the questions. What will happen:

- if the electricity isn't on?
- if there's no filter paper inside?
- if you don't put in enough coffee?
- if you don't pour in enough water?
- if the coffee pot isn't under the filter?
- if the red light doesn't go on?
- if you don't want your coffee immediately?

Example: If the electricity <u>isn't</u> on, the machine <u>won't</u> work.

5 Read and connect ideas. Put these instructions for a dishwasher in the right order.

A Place the dirty dishes in the racks.
B Close the door.
C Plug in the machine.
D Pull out the racks.
E Place glasses, cups and saucepans upside down.
F Pour a cupful of detergent in the bottom of the machine.
G The machine starts to fill up with water.
H Leave it there until you need it.
I Press the switch. The red light goes on.
J Push the racks back in the machine.
K Open the door.
L Turn on the electricity.
M After about an hour, the noise stops. Take out the clean washing-up.
N Turn the switch to the programme you require.

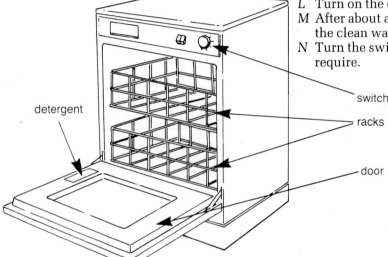

detergent

switch

racks

door

6 Now join the sentences into pairs, using *then*, *when* and *as soon as*. Use the passage in 3 to help you.

Examples: Plug in the machine, and then turn on the electricity.

When		stops,	
As soon as	the noise	has stopped,	take out the clean washing-up.

7 Write questions about the dishwasher like the questions about the coffee machine in 4.

Example: – What <u>will</u> happen if you <u>don't</u> close the door?
– It <u>won't</u> work.

Now work in pairs. Ask questions about the dishwasher and answer your partner's questions.

8 Write instructions on how to do something. Here are some ideas:

How to:
- use a cassette recorder
- use a washing machine
- buy a bus ticket in your town
- cash a cheque in a bank
- boil an egg
- give a dog a bath

9 Describe your instructions to your partner, but do not say what they are for. He/she must try and guess what the instructions are for.

Work in groups of two or three.

GROUP A

10   Discuss what will happen if:

- there are sharks about
- the brakes on your car don't work
- you're in a room full of smoke

Example: If the brakes on your car don't work,
             you won't be able to stop.

11   Read and connect ideas. Here are some instructions on how to survive in the dangerous situations. Complete each sentence with two instructions.

Sharks are attracted by light things, so . . .
Your safety is more important than your car,
    so . . .
There is always five centimetres of clearer air
    above the floor, so . . .

. . . cover your arms and legs.
. . . slow down by driving off the road or
    alongside a wall.
. . . put a wet cloth over your mouth.
. . . wear dark clothing.
. . . change to first gear even if you're moving
    fast.
. . . go down on your hands and knees.

Example: Sharks are attracted by light things,
             so wear dark clothing and . . .

12   Rewrite the sentences using *because*.

Example: . . . and wear dark clothing, because
             sharks are attracted by light things.

Can you think of any other instructions for the situations? Write similar sentences using *so* or *because*.

13   Now think about what you do if:
- there are bears about
- you have to jump out of a window upstairs
- you're caught in quicksand

14   Check your answers with Group B. Find out what they think about your situations. Ask them why.

GROUP **B**

10 **Discuss what will happen if:**

- there are bears about
- you have to jump out of a window upstairs
- you're caught in quicksand

Example: If there are bears about, they'll chase you.

11 **Read and connect ideas. Here are some instructions on how to survive in the dangerous situations. Complete each sentence with two instructions.**

Remember that bears like food and have shorter
   front legs than back legs, so . . .
Even jumping from the first floor can be
   dangerous, so . . .
Some quicksand is strong enough to support a
   little weight for a short time, so . . .

. . . climb down sheets as far as possible.
. . . lie down on something like a coat, beach
   towel or air bed.
. . . try to escape by running downhill.
. . . throw mattresses and cushions to soften the
   landing.
. . . don't attract them with your picnic baskets.
. . . try to run across it.

Example: Remember that bears like food and
   have shorter front legs than back
   legs, so don't attract them with your
   picnic baskets and . . .

12 **Rewrite the sentences using *because*.**

Example: . . . and don't attract them with
   your picnic baskets, because bears
   like food.

Can you think of any other instructions for the situations? Write similar sentences using *so* or *because*.

13 **Now think about what you do if:**
- there are sharks about
- the brakes on your car don't work
- you're in a room full of smoke

14 **Check your answers with Group A. Find out what they think about your situations. Ask them why.**

15 **Work in groups of two or three. Think of instructions on what to do if:**

- you discover a fire in your school
- you're caught in a snow/sand storm while driving in your car
- you get lost in the mountains in bad weather
- you are on a desert island with twenty people and only enough food for ten

Discuss your instructions with other groups. Make a list of the four most important instructions for each situation. Make sure you explain why.

16 **Write sentences giving your instructions for two situations.**

Pronunciation and Structure Review: page 157.

22 Describing changes

1   Read and connect ideas. Decide where these sentences should go in the dialogue on the right.

- I didn't like wearing school uniform
- we used to do as children
- it used to be straight
- I didn't use to be so slim either
- Did you use to have short hair
- what kind of clothes did you wear

JEAN: Do you remember the other day, we were talking about what . . . ?
BILL: Yes, I remember. Why?
JEAN: Well, I've found a photo taken when I was twelve years old.
BILL: Oh, can I see?
JEAN: Yes, hang on a minute. It's here somewhere.
BILL: . . . ?
JEAN: No, very long hair. And . . . .
BILL: And . . . ?
JEAN: Mostly jeans and sweat-shirts . . . . Actually, I really wanted to be a boy. And . . . . In fact, I used to be a little, well, chubby! Oh, here it is! Just look at those freckles!

🔲 **Listen and check.**

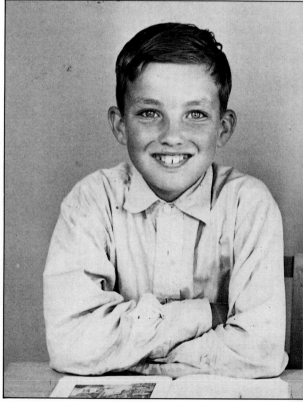

2   Work in pairs. Look at the photo of Bill when he was a child. Say what he used to look like.

Example: He used to have short hair.

3   Work in pairs. Ask and tell each other what you looked like when you were children. Use the dialogue in 1 to help you.

What did you look like? Did you use to . . . ?	I	used didn't use	to . . .

**4 Predict before listening.
You are going to hear Bill and
Jean talking about their
childhood. Here are some of
the topics they may mention.
Write down some of the
questions they may ask each
other.**

- home
- family
- friends
- games and hobbies
- school
- holidays

Examples: Where did you use
to live?
Did you use to go
to school nearby?

**5 [cassette] Listen for main ideas.
Which of the topics in 4 do Bill
and Jean mention? Did you
hear any of your questions?**

6 [cassette] Listen for specific information. Work in pairs.

STUDENT A

**Listen again and write notes on what Bill says
about his childhood.**

STUDENT B

**Listen again and write notes on what Jean
says about her childhood.**

7 Work together. Now compare Bill's and Jean's childhood.

Examples: She used to have very long hair, but his hair used to be very short.
He used to live in the country, whereas she used to live in the town.
He didn't use to like school, while she used to love it.

**8 Tell other students about your childhood. Use the topics in 4 to help you. Form groups of two or
three. Find two things about your childhood which were the same.**

Example: We both/all used to live in a city.

Now find two things about your childhood which were different.

Example: Peter used to hate school, whereas André and Lee used to like it.

9 Write sentences describing what you had in common, and what was different.

93

**10 Look at the statements below and complete
the chart for your country. If you agree, put a tick
(✔). If you disagree, put a cross (✘).
If you don't know, put a question mark (?).**

YOUR COUNTRY Today	BRITAIN Today	BRITAIN 50 years ago

1   Most families have at least four children.

2   Lots of families have servants.

3   Most women go out to work.

4   Children don't leave school until they're sixteen.

5   Most people find a job when they leave school.

6   People often go out in the evenings.

7   The cinema is very popular.

8   Most people have cars.

9   People travel a lot.

10 Many people spend their whole life in their home town.

11 🔲 **Listen for main ideas. Here are two people talking about life in Britain today and fifty
years ago. Put a tick in the boxes in 10 if they agree with the statements and a cross if they disagree.**

12 Work in pairs. Take turns to compare life in Britain fifty years ago with today.

Examples: The school leaving age used to be fourteen, <u>while</u> today it's sixteen.
            It used to be quite easy to find a job, but it <u>isn't any more</u>.

13 Now compare life in Britain today with life in your country.

Example: Families in Britain are quite small, <u>whereas</u> in my country they are quite large.

14   Read for main ideas. Choose the best title for this passage.

HOLIDAYS   MY CHILDHOOD MEMORIES   CHILDREN IN BRITAIN   FAMILY LIFE

I remember the cold winters most of all. When we got up there used to be ice on the windows. My mother always gave me and my brother an egg for breakfast in winter to help us keep warm. But we had to wear short trousers for school and my knees used to go red, especially if there was a strong wind. The classrooms weren't very warm, and sometimes we stayed cold all day! On Saturday mornings we went to the cinema–I used to look forward to that all week. There were special films for children while our parents went shopping. It was great fun! We always spent our holidays by the sea, sometimes in Devon, sometimes on the Isle of Wight. We spent all the time in the water or making sand castles. I always think the sun used to shine all the time. Sunday was the nicest day of the week. We usually had roast beef or lamb for lunch, and my parents used to have a glass of wine while my brother and I had lemonade. We spent the afternoon in the garden, perhaps burning the leaves in the autumn or cutting the grass in summer. We used to have tea and then I had a bath. Anything else? Oh yes, my dog. I used to take him for a walk every day and at the weekends we spent all morning in the park. He died when I was sixteen. That's when I think my childhood finished.

15   Read for main ideas. List the five topics the writer describes as he remembers his childhood.

16   Build your vocabulary. Look at the passage and find:

- four things to do with the weather
- three meals
- three things to eat
- three times of the year

17   Read and connect ideas. Decide where these sentences should go in the passage.

A We used to stay in a guest house, a kind of small, cheap hotel.
B I'm sure I had more than one bath a week, but Sunday bathtime is the only one I remember now!
C My school was about five miles away and I used to walk to the bus stop every day, getting colder and colder!

18   Think of four or five childhood memories and tell your partner about them. Then write a paragraph describing your memories. Use the passage in 14 to help you.

Pronunciation and Structure Review: page 159.

Finding things out

1 📼 **Listen for main ideas. David is checking arrangements with Kathy for the next part of their trip today. Listen and note down any corrections to make to his notes.**

> 40 mile drive. 2 hours ??
>
> Hotel booked in Colombo.
>
> Interview arranged for tomorrow morning. Phone secretary to fix time.

2 Look at the way question tags link up with the rest of the sentence.

> It's 40 miles, isn't it?
> He knew the number, didn't he?
> It shouldn't take long, should it?
> She hasn't lost the map, has she?

Now complete David's statements in the dialogue below with the following question tags:

- aren't we?
- haven't we?
- didn't you?
- should it?
- can't I?
- have you?

DAVID:	So we've got about two hours drive before we get to Colombo, . . .
KATHY:	. . . .
DAVID:	And we're staying in a hotel there, . . .
KATHY:	. . . .
DAVID:	Oh, you did that last week, . . .
KATHY:	. . . .
DAVID:	OK. And you haven't arranged the interview too early tomorrow, . . .
KATHY:	. . . .
DAVID:	Oh yes, that's right. I can call him from the hotel, . . . I thought we might try to see him in the morning. That shouldn't be too difficult to organise, . . .
KATHY:	. . . .

3 Kathy's replies are in reported speech below. They are in the wrong order. First, decide where her replies go in the dialogue.

Kathy said:
- she hadn't arranged the interview yet. Mr Clarke knew about it. But David was going to phone Mr Clarke's secretary that night.
- Mr Clarke was busy the next morning.
- she had tried to ring, but there had been no answer. But it was no problem, because there were plenty of hotels in Colombo.
- the drive would take about three hours. It was about fifty miles.
- they hadn't booked their rooms.

4 Now think about what Kathy actually says. Write down her exact words.

 Listen and check.

Example: She said the drive <u>would</u> take about three hours.
'The drive <u>will</u> take about three hours, actually,' she said.

5 Work in pairs and act out the dialogue. Make sure your intonation rises on the question tags.

6 On the way to Colombo, David and his companions had an accident. Discuss with your partner what you think happened.

7 Read the police report of the accident. Then write the policeman's questions.

POLICE REPORT

I asked the driver of the jeep who he was and what he did. Mr David Piper replied that he was a radio producer for the BBC. He said that he lived in London and that he was going to Colombo. He said that he and his colleagues had been in Sri Lanka for two weeks, and had an appointment to interview Mr Arthur C. Clarke. He said that the mini-bus overtook their jeep. It then slowed down, probably because of the difficult road and Mr Piper's jeep hit it. Mr Silva, the other driver, said that he overtook because Mr Piper was driving very slowly. Suddenly Mr Piper's jeep started to go faster and then it hit Mr Silva's mini-bus.

Examples: Can you tell me where you live?
Do you know what happened?

Can you tell me Do you know Have you any idea	where when what who how long why	. . . ?

8 Work in pairs. Act out the conversation between David and the policeman. Use the police report to help you.

9 Arthur C. Clarke is famous for his predictions about the future. He is also well known for his interest in mysterious events and things that are difficult to explain. The sentences opposite are from a report on a radio talk given by Dr Roger Johns on Arthur C. Clarke's *Mysterious World*. The sections are not in the right order.

Deal with difficult vocabulary. Read the sentences and write down any words you don't know. Look at each word.

- What type of word is it?
- Can you guess its general sense from the rest of the passage?
- Ask another student if he/she knows what it means.

You can look up five words in your dictionary. Make sure you choose them carefully.

A In his talk Dr Johns said that, according to Clarke, there were three types of mystery. A Mystery of the First Kind was usually something in the natural world which people once found extraordinary, such as rainbows.

B But Mysteries of the Third Kind were the most strange, because there was no explanation at all. As a result, there was very little to say about them.

C Every day people were finding new explanations for these mysteries, but no one had found the one and only answer. After a while, most Mysteries of the Second Kind were solved and became Mysteries of the First Kind.

D An example of this last type was when objects were thrown around for no physical reason. This was one of many Mysteries of the Third Kind which people simply refused to believe.

E But scientists could now explain them. Mysteries of the Second Kind were still mysteries, like Unidentified Flying Objects or the Loch Ness Monster.

10 Read and connect ideas. Put the sections in the right order. The first section is A.

11  Listen and check your answer to 10. As you listen, try to remember what the tenses of the verbs are.

Now rewrite the sentences as if Dr Johns was speaking. Start like this:

'According to Arthur C. Clarke, there <u>are</u> three types of mystery. . . .'

12 Predict before reading. Look at the cartoons, which illustrate the three stories below. What do you think each story is likely to be about?

13 Read for main ideas. Match the stories with the cartoons.

1 On 19th May 1780, between ten o'clock and eleven o'clock in the morning, darkness covered the whole of New England in the USA and lasted for a whole day. Many people thought it was the end of the world. But a scientist, Mr Samuel Williams, discovered that it was caused by forest fires in Vermont.

2 On 30th December 1978, a film crew in a plane saw a bright light in the sky over New Zealand, and they filmed it. The bright object flew beside the plane for some time. When the film was shown on television, people said the light came from Jupiter, Venus, Japanese fishing boats, or was simply caused by the weather.

3 In England, in 1919, an author called J. Temple Thurston died in his living room in Kent. No one could explain how the lower part of his body was burnt when there was no sign of fire in the room and the rest of his body was untouched, or how his body burnt without damaging his clothes.

14 ▣ Listen for detail. Note down any differences between what Dr Johns says and the stories in 13.

Now work in pairs. Say what the differences are.

Example: In the story, it said that the forest fires were in Vermont. But Dr Johns said . . .

15 Put the last part of the talk into reported speech. Make sure you change the tenses of the verbs.

'Mysteries of the First Kind aren't mysteries at all any more, but they amazed and frightened people at the time. As for Mysteries of the Second Kind, there's always a simple explanation. Unfortunately we don't know what it is. And there are some mysteries which we'll never be able to understand. That's why they're Mysteries of the Third Kind. But all three kinds of mysteries are fun and add to our enjoyment of the world about us.'

Begin: Dr Johns said that Mysteries of the First Kind were not mysteries at all any more, but they amazed and frightened people at the time . . .

Pronunciation and Structure Review: page 160.

Unit 24 Checking what you know

1   Look at the photograph and decide which of the foods are good for your health, and which are not. Make two lists.

2   [cassette] **Listen for specific information.** Listen to Annie and Robert talking about healthy eating. Check your answers to 1.

3   Ask and say what you should and shouldn't eat if you want to be healthy, and explain why.

> You should eat a lot of . . . because . . .

> . . . is/are bad for you, so you shouldn't eat too much of it/many of them.

4   Work in pairs. Find out about your partner's diet.

How much/many . . . do you eat?	I don't eat much/many . . . I only eat a little/a few . . . I eat a lot of . . . I eat too much/many . . . I don't eat enough . . .

5   Write a few sentences comparing your diet with your partner's.

Examples: He eats more cheese than I do.
I don't eat as much sugar as she does.
I eat lots of fruit, whereas he eats more vegetables.

6 Work in pairs. Look at some of the things David has taken with him on his trip to Sri Lanka. Choose one item and describe it to your partner in as much detail as possible, but do not say which one it is.

Say: ● what size, shape or colour it is
 ● how heavy, big or long it is
 ● where it's from (if you know), what it's made of and what it's for

Your partner must try to decide which object you are describing. Change roles when you have finished.

7  Listen for detail. The shape below is a room in Jean's flat. Copy it, and then listen to her describing what is in the room. Complete your drawing with all the furniture, fittings and equipment in the right position.

Compare and check your drawing with that of another student.

8   Read and connect ideas. Look at the instructions below and put them in the right order.

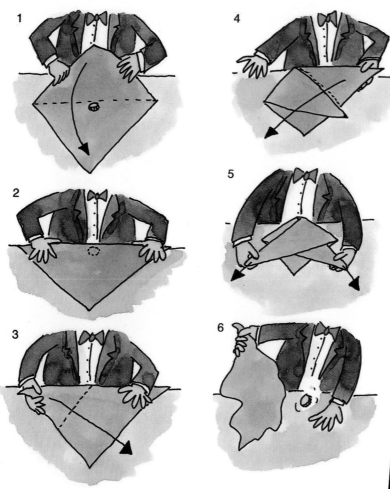

SIMPLY MAGIC

The Hungry Handkerc...

Here's a magic trick to am...
your friends, and all you n...
is a coin and a handkerch...

A   Make sure the coin is tuc...
in tightly and tell your
audience that the
handkerchief is now eatin...
the coin. Now take one of
the loose ends in each han...
and PULL – the coin will
appear to have disappeare...
(It's actually held in the fo...
along the top edge.)

B   Place the open handkerchi...
on a table and place the coi...
in the middle.

C   Fold the handkerchief in
half to make a triangle,
making sure the coin stays i...
the middle of the fold.

D   . . . then fold the left-hand
corner across to the right.

E   Now crumple the
handkerchief into one of
your hands, lift it and the
coin will magically
reappear!

F   Now carefully fold the right-
hand corner across to the left
as in the picture . . .

Check your answer with another student.

9   Try and do the trick.
Do you know any other magic tricks, or games to play? Tell your
partner about them.

**10   Write brief instructions on how to do something. Here are
some ideas:**

● how to make a phone call from a public telephone in your country
● how to make an omelette
● how to get a taxi in your country
● how to get to London from your country

As you write the instructions, leave out five key words.

Example: You pick up the . . . and you wait for the . . . . Then you . . . the number.
When someone . . . , you . . . some money in and speak.

Now give your instructions to your partner who must read them and guess what they are for.

11 Work in pairs. What are the differences between life today and life at the beginning of the century? Think about the following:

- food
- a typical day
- clothes
- leisure activities
- work
- transport

Make a list of the differences, and then compare your list with other students.

Example: They used to eat more than we do today.

12 Work in pairs.

STUDENT A

Check that Student B:

- was born in June
- isn't married
- lives in London
- will lend you five pounds
- can't swim

STUDENT B

Check that Student A:

- was born in December
- is a doctor
- doesn't smoke
- won't be late tomorrow
- can speak fluent English

Use the exchange below as a model.

– You were born in June, weren't you?
– Yes, I was./No, I wasn't. I was born in May.

Think of three more things to check about each other.

13 Now write a short report on what your partner said.

Example: I asked him if he was born in June. He said that he was born in May.

14 Build your vocabulary. Look back over Units 19 to 23, and write ten words in each of the categories below.

KITCHEN EQUIPMENT   FOOD   TRANSPORT

Talking about the future (1)

1 Build your vocabulary. Look at this photograph. How many of these features can you see? Use your dictionary if necessary.

road	mountain	hill
river	village	jungle
fence	hedge	bridge
valley	field	desert
beach	forest	path
sea	lake	tree

Work in pairs and check. Which of the other features do you expect to find in Scotland? Which of them do you find in your country?

2 Predict before reading. Look at the title of the passage on page 105 and guess what it is about. Write down five words you expect to see in the passage.

3 Read and infer. First read the statements below. Then read the passage on page 105, and decide if the statements are true or false. If they are false, discuss with another student what the passage actually says.

1 The acid rain problem is unlikely to get worse.
2 Black snow is likely to become more common.
3 Highland forests won't die.
4 The fish will certainly die.
5 Acid in the water might kill food supplies.
6 The birds will probably disappear.
7 Scotland has lost its tourist industry.
8 Tourists will certainly stay away if the countryside is destroyed.

Example: 1 *False.* The acid rain problem is unlikely to get better.

. . . will certainly	=	. . . is/are certain to
. . . will probably	=	. . . is/are likely to
. . . will possibly	=	. . . may/might/could
. . . probably won't	=	. . . is/are unlikely to
. . . certainly won't		

4 Complete these sentences to make true statements about the effects of pollution.

1 The acid rain problem is . . . to get better.
2 Black snow will . . . become more common.
3 Highland forests . . . probably die.
4 The fish probably . . . be able to live in the rivers.
5 Acid in the water is . . . to kill food supplies.
6 The birds are . . . to disappear.
7 Scotland will . . . lose its tourist industry.
8 Tourists . . . won't come if the countryside is destroyed.

THE BEAUTY OF SCOTLAND – HOW LONG WILL IT LAST?

The Scottish Highlands have some of the most beautiful scenery in the world. Until now, Scotland has escaped much of the pollution which affects Western Europe. But it may not escape for much longer.

The problem is acid rain.

Cars and power stations that burn coal cause acid rain. It isn't always rain; sometimes it's a mist which falls on trees, buildings and the ground. And it is increasing.

In parts of Western Europe the problem is serious. Experts think that over half of the forests in West Germany are dying. Acid rain has damaged over forty per cent of Dutch forests, and poisoned 18,000 Swedish lakes.

Until recently, the wind carried away most of Britain's acid rain, usually towards Scandinavia. The British Government was not particularly interested in a form of pollution which came from Britain but which only seemed to affect other countries. But there's so much acid rain now that it falls on Britain.

In 1974, during a storm over Pitlochry, the rain contained so much acid that it was like vinegar. On 20th February 1984, black snow fell at Aviemore in the Cairngorm Mountains. Local people say it happens often. In Edinburgh and Glasgow some of the older buildings are very badly damaged. In Loch Enoch and Loch Fleet there are no longer any fish at all.

And the situation is unlikely to get better. As the trees disappear from mountain slopes, avalanches will probably increase. The chemicals in acid rain are likely to replace the oxygen in lakes and rivers. The fish are unlikely to live, because the acid in the water will certainly kill their young and their food supplies, such as water insects. Birds and animals will probably disappear when they no longer have anything to feed on.

The consequences are economic as well. Scotland may lose its tourist industry. The tourists certainly won't come to rivers which have lost their salmon and trout, or to scenery which has lost its beauty. And without the money the tourists bring, the Highlanders might have to go elsewhere to find work.

Unless the British Government does something soon, acid rain will change the face of the Scottish countryside – and the lives of the people who live there.

5   Build your vocabulary. There may be some more words you do not understand. You can look up four of them in your dictionary. Make sure you choose the words carefully.

6   Read for specific information. Describe the consequences of pollution in Scotland.

If	power stations continue to burn coal, acid rain falls on forests, the trees disappear, acid rain falls on lakes and rivers, the oxygen is replaced by chemicals, there are no water insects, the fish disappear, the government does nothing,	. . . will . . .

Example: If power stations <u>continue</u> to burn coal, acid rain <u>will increase</u>.

7   Write a short paragraph about the consequences of pollution in Scotland. Use your answers in 6 to help you.

Begin: Unless power stations stop burning coal, acid rain will increase. If it falls on the forests . . .

8 Build your vocabulary. This section is about politics. Which of the following words are you likely to see?

government	minister
river	state
vote	president
cheque	cabinet
representative	power
conservative	socialist
computer	election
airline	parliament
political	party
saucepan	general

9 Read and infer. Look at the article below, and complete the chart for Britain.

ELECTION FEVER

Most British politicians spend a great deal of time discussing when the next general election will be. In the House of Commons, they talk about it all the time. Members of Parliament know that if they don't get enough votes they could be looking for a new job.

In Britain, for many years, the contest has been between the Conservative Party on the right, and the Labour Party on the left. But there are now two other major political parties in the centre: the Social Democrats and the Liberals. And of course, the centre parties hope to attract more votes from both conservatives and socialists.

The British Head of State is not a president; it is a king or queen who has little real power. One of the few important functions left to the Head of State is to make sure that the Head of Government, the Prime Minister, calls a general election within five years. The PM listens to the advice of the cabinet ministers, and chooses a time when public opinion is favourable. At last the date of the general election is announced and the voters, who must be over the age of eighteen, make their choice. And as soon as it is all over, the politicians start talking about when the next election will be.

	BRITAIN	YOUR COUNTRY
1 What is the Head of State called?		
2 What is the Head of Government called?		
3 What are the major political parties called?		
4 What are the elected representatives called?		
5 Where do the elected representatives meet?		
6 From what age can people vote?		

Now fill in the chart for your country.

10 Build your vocabulary. Find five words which can be nouns or adjectives.

Example: conservative

Find five words which refer to groups of people.

Example: state

11 🔲 Listen for main ideas. You are going to hear an interview with a British politician. How much does he think things are likely to change? For each statement below, write down the letter which corresponds to his degree of certainty.

A Certain *B* Likely/Probable *C* Possible *D* Not sure/Don't know *E* Unlikely *F* Impossible

1 A president will replace the monarch in Britain.
2 There will be general elections every three years.
3 There will be more and more different political parties.
4 People will be allowed to vote when they're sixteen.
5 Members of Parliament will stop work when they're sixty-five.

12 Check your answers with another student. Write sentences saying what is or is not likely to change in Britain, according to the politician.

Example: A president probably won't replace the Queen in Britain.

13 Work in pairs. Make five predictions about politics in your country *or* about international politics and write them in a chart.

Now discuss your predictions with other students and find out what they think. Do not show them your chart. Put a letter A – F according to how likely they think your predictions are.

Examples:

Predictions	André	Justine	Maria
There'll be a woman president in the USA soon.	D	B	E
Our government will stay in power for ten years.	F	E	D

I think there'll be a woman president in the USA soon.
I don't think the government will lose the election.
What do you think will happen to the Conservatives?

	Agreeing	Disagreeing
I think . . . will . . .	So do I. I think so, too.	Well, I don't think so. No, . . . won't!
I don't think . . . will . . .	Nor/Neither do I. I don't think so, either.	Well, I think . . . will. Yes, . . . will!

Pronunciation and Structure Review: page 161.

Talking about the future (2)

1 📼 **Listen for main ideas. Work in pairs. Jean has just seen some of her clients. Listen to Jean's conversation with Bill and match the clients' names with the problems.**

Name	Problem	Action to be taken
Mr Campbell		
Mr and Mrs Seymour		
Mr Smith		
Mr and Mrs Field		
Mrs Holmes		
Mrs Keith		
Mr Thomas		
Mr and Mrs Lane		

1 room too noisy
2 lost passport
3 don't like the food
4 room has no bath
5 want to fly home a week later
6 feels ill
7 lost wallet
8 too hot in room

📼 **Now listen again and check. Can you make any other suggestions?**

> I suggest she . . .
> If I were Jean, I'd . . .
> I think she should . . .
> I think she could . . .
> Perhaps she could . . .
> She'd better . . .

2 Predict before listening. Match each problem with the action to be taken below. Be careful! There are some extra suggestions.

A move to a room away from the disco
B phone the airline, change ticket
C ring their family in England
D have a good look and then contact the Consulate
E ask to see a plumber
F go to the police
G telephone the doctor
H turn the heating up
I move to a room with a bath
J turn up the air conditioning
K tell them about the nightclubs
L ask for simpler dishes

3 Role play. Work in pairs.

> STUDENT A
>
> You are Bill.
>
> **Offer to do things in the list in 2.**

> STUDENT B
>
> You are Jean.
>
> **Choose four things in the list in 2 which you will do. Now accept or refuse Bill's offers to do things.**

I'll . . .	OK, thank you very much.
Shall I . . . ?	No, it's all right. I'll do that.

4 Read and connect ideas. Jean has received this note from Bill. Think about Jean's reply by choosing some sentences from the list below.

Dear Bill,
it sounds a wonderful idea
I'm afraid I'm busy on Friday
I'd love to come with you
I think it'll take all day
I have to write some letters
what time shall we meet
perhaps we could take a picnic
I think I could come later
it won't take all day
I suggest we leave at nine o'clock
why don't we choose another day
thank you for your note
in the morning
in the afternoon
I'd love to come another time
I'm very busy at the moment
I want to do some shopping
I really can't say when I'll be free
Yours,
Jean

Dear Jean,
I didn't have a chance to ask you last night, but I was wondering if you were doing anything on Friday. If you are free, why don't we go somewhere together? We have to collect some people from the airport at 6 p.m. but I think we could easily spend the day on the beach. Perhaps we could leave early in the morning and drive up the coast to a fishing village I know? I suggest we have lunch in a restaurant somewhere and perhaps have a look at the port there. Then we could go swimming and lie in the sun for a few hours in the afternoon. How about it?
Yours,
Bill.

5 Now write Jean's reply using the phrases you have chosen. Add *but*, *and*, *so* and punctuation where necessary.

6 Work in pairs. Think of two or three things to do in each situation.

- Your car won't start and you have a plane to catch.
- You've left your bath running, but the bathroom door won't open.
- You've arrived at your friend's house for dinner, but the doorbell won't ring.
- You phone the police because of a noise downstairs at night, but they won't answer your call.
- Your dog ate your English homework, but your teacher won't believe you.
- You need a lot of money, but your bank won't lend you any.
- Your neighbours like loud music and they won't turn it down.
- You lent a book to a friend but he refuses to give it back.

Make suggestions about what you could do.

I suggest we . . .
Perhaps we could . . .
I think we should . . .
Why don't we . . . ?
How/What about . . . ?
Let's . . .

7 Think of two more difficult situations.
Now tell other students about them. What do they suggest you should do?

8 Think about things to do on your free day this week. Make suggestions and invitations to other students by writing them notes. Reply to the suggestions you receive. Use Bill's and Jean's notes in 4 to help you.

9 Read and connect ideas. Work in pairs. The paragraphs below come from Chapter 1 of a story called *Promises, Promises*. Read them and put them in the right order.

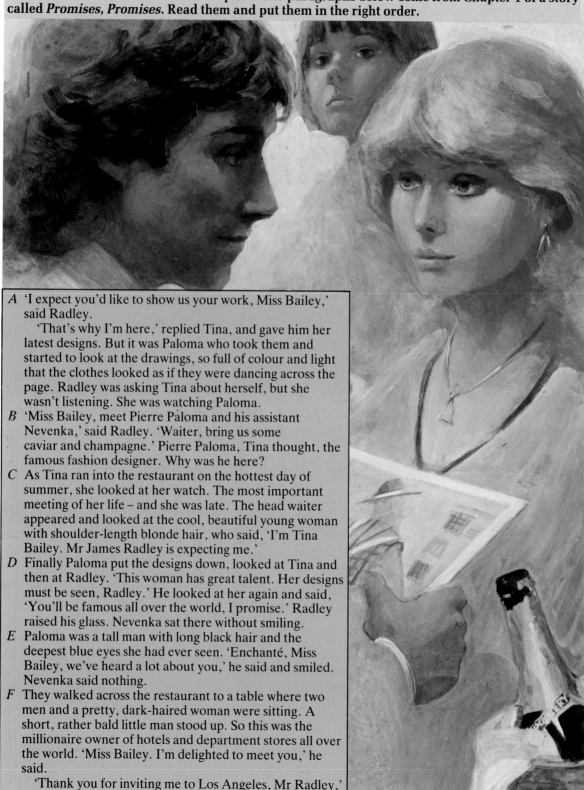

A 'I expect you'd like to show us your work, Miss Bailey,' said Radley.
   'That's why I'm here,' replied Tina, and gave him her latest designs. But it was Paloma who took them and started to look at the drawings, so full of colour and light that the clothes looked as if they were dancing across the page. Radley was asking Tina about herself, but she wasn't listening. She was watching Paloma.

B 'Miss Bailey, meet Pierre Paloma and his assistant Nevenka,' said Radley. 'Waiter, bring us some caviar and champagne.' Pierre Paloma, Tina thought, the famous fashion designer. Why was he here?

C As Tina ran into the restaurant on the hottest day of summer, she looked at her watch. The most important meeting of her life – and she was late. The head waiter appeared and looked at the cool, beautiful young woman with shoulder-length blonde hair, who said, 'I'm Tina Bailey. Mr James Radley is expecting me.'

D Finally Paloma put the designs down, looked at Tina and then at Radley. 'This woman has great talent. Her designs must be seen, Radley.' He looked at her again and said, 'You'll be famous all over the world, I promise.' Radley raised his glass. Nevenka sat there without smiling.

E Paloma was a tall man with long black hair and the deepest blue eyes she had ever seen. 'Enchanté, Miss Bailey, we've heard a lot about you,' he said and smiled. Nevenka said nothing.

F They walked across the restaurant to a table where two men and a pretty, dark-haired woman were sitting. A short, rather bald little man stood up. So this was the millionaire owner of hotels and department stores all over the world. 'Miss Bailey. I'm delighted to meet you,' he said.
   'Thank you for inviting me to Los Angeles, Mr Radley,' said Tina.

10 Predict before listening. Here are some phrases from Chapter 2 of the story. Discuss what you think this part of the story is likely to be about.

three months since the meeting
nothing had happened
fashion show in Smeralda next spring
biggest department store in Milan
Nevenka was out of the room
I'll be in London next month. I'll call you
phone rang

everything is arranged
doing nothing on Saturday
spent a wonderful autumn day together
sun was going down as they walked along the beach
I couldn't come over last month. I can't explain
kissed her

Listen and check.

11 Work in pairs.

STUDENT A

Cover Student B's section. Read your part of Chapter 3. Tell Student B about your part of the chapter.

In the winter months, Tina and her assistants were getting everything ready for the fashion show in Milan. Radley had said, 'I'll invite all the fashion journalists and the richest customers.' Tina yawned. In three weeks she had had only one full night's sleep. It was hard work, but a happy time. Except for one thing: Pierre hadn't rung.

One day she decided to ring him.

STUDENT B

Cover Student A's section. Read your part of Chapter 3. Listen to Student A telling you about part of the chapter. Then tell Student A about your part of the chapter.

Nevenka answered the phone. She said Pierre was much too busy to talk to Tina.

In the spring, Tina flew to Milan. She was nervous that no one would come to the fashion show or that no one would like her dresses. At the airport, she made sure the woman van driver from Smeralda packed the dresses properly. Then she took a taxi to Smeralda and waited. She waited and waited.

12 Say what Pierre Paloma and Radley promise Tina:

- famous all over the world
- fashion show in Smeralda next spring
- call her
- fashion show a great success
- all the fashion journalists as well as the richest customers

Example: Pierre promises she'll be famous all over the world.

13 Predict before listening. Try to guess how the story will end.

Listen and check.

14 Work in pairs. Discuss with your partner how the story will end. Think about these points:
- What will happen at the fashion show? Will Tina's dresses be a great success?

- Will Tina be famous all over the world? Will her life change?

- Will Pierre keep his promises? What will happen to Tina and Pierre? Will they get married, or will Tina say goodbye?

Now write the last three paragraphs of the story, based on your answers to the questions above.

Pronunciation and Structure Review: page 162.

Discussing future possibilities

1   Predict before reading. Arthur C. Clarke is a famous science-fiction writer, best known for his work on the film *2001: A Space Odyssey*. Which of the following words are you likely to find in his biography?

wrote	manufactured	drove	born
started	presented	voted	built
danced	published	painted	lived

Now write down five more words which you are likely to find.

2   Read for specific information. Read Arthur C. Clarke's biography and find the answers to the following questions.

1   When did he start writing science fiction?
2   What was *2001: A Space Odyssey* based on?
3   Who did he write *2001: A Space Odyssey* with?
4   What did he do at the time of the first moon landing?
5   Where was *2010* written?
6   What is *The Fountains of Paradise* about?

CLARKE, Arthur C. (b. 1917)

Clarke was born in Somerset, England, but has lived mostly in Sri Lanka since 1957. He started writing science fiction at school and continued when he joined the Civil Service at the age of nineteen. Since then, many of the predictions he has made in his stories have become science fact. In 1938 he predicted the possibility of 'Star Wars'. Seven years later he published an article explaining how satellites could be used for communication networks in the future. In 1951 he wrote the short story, *The Sentinel*, and this was the main source for the film *2001: A Space Odyssey*, released seventeen years later, which he wrote with the film director Stanley Kubrick. In the late 1960s, he spent much time in America lecturing about the space age. He was a commentator on American television when the first pictures of men on the moon were broadcast in 1969. *2010*, the sequel to the film *2001*, was written in the 1970s with Peter Hyams, who worked in Hollywood, while Clarke stayed in Sri Lanka. In 1979 he published *The Fountains of Paradise*, a science fiction story set in Sri Lanka about a man who wants to build a 'space elevator'. In 1983 he presented a television series, *The Mysterious World*.

3   ▣▣ Listen for main ideas. Here is David Piper's introduction to a BBC radio programme on Arthur C. Clarke. You will then hear four passages taken from the interview in which Clarke talks about his life and work. Listen and choose a heading for each passage from the list below. Be careful! There are some extra headings.

A   Co-writing *2001: A Space Odyssey*
B   Childhood influences on his writing
C   Time of the moon landing
D   Influence of Sri Lanka on his writing
E   Co-writing *2010*

F   Future plans
G   His move to Sri Lanka
H   His first job
I   Writing *The Sentinel*

4   Put the four passage headings in the order they happened in Arthur C. Clarke's life.

5  **Listen for main ideas. Here is Arthur C. Clarke talking about what he does during a typical working day. Which things does he mention?**

A wakes up
B goes for a swim
C has tea in bed
D listens to the radio
E has breakfast
F goes for a walk
G reads the newspaper
H starts work
I has lunch
J sees friends
K plays table tennis
L has dinner
M watches television
N goes to bed

6 **Listen for specific information. Listen again and say when he does the things in 5. Choose from the list of times below.**

6 a.m.	2 p.m.
6.30 a.m.	4 p.m.
7 a.m.	4.30 p.m.
7.30 a.m.	6 p.m.
8.30 a.m.	6.30 p.m.
9 a.m.	7 p.m.
11 a.m.	9 p.m.
12 noon	10.30 p.m.

7 **Write a description of Arthur C. Clarke's day. Use your answers to 5 and 6 and the outline below to help you.**

Arthur C. Clarke . . . at . . . and . . . bed. He . . . ten minutes, and then he gets up . . . . He starts . . . and . . . noon. At about . . . in the afternoon, he goes to the local club . . . . After that, he goes home to . . . the BBC news at . . . , and . . . . Then he works until . . . , when he . . . .

8 **If you were rich and famous like Arthur C. Clarke, would you spend your day in the same way? Find three things you would do the same as him, and three things you would not do.**

Examples: I'd work, but I wouldn't start work so early.
I'd have lunch at 12 o'clock.
I wouldn't play table tennis.

9 **Describe your typical day if you were very rich and famous. Tell your partner about it. Use the list in 5 to help you.**

10   Read and connect ideas. Put the paragraphs about the film *2001: A Space Odyssey* in order.

An epic drama of adventure and exploratic

MGM PRESENTS A STANLEY KUBRICK PRODUCTION

2001
Space
Odyssey
U

r Panavision®
Metrocolor

MGM

2001: A Space Odyssey

METRO–GOLDWYN–MAYER

Produced by Stanley Kubrick; screenplay by Stanley Kubrick and Arthur C. Clarke from Clarke's short story *The Sentinel*; directed by Stanley Kubrick.

A Alone in space, the last part of David's journey becomes more spiritual as he approaches Jupiter. At the end of his journey, he sees himself in rooms of surreal beauty, growing older as he moves away from Earth. Finally, we see David become an unborn child again, returning to his origins as he floats in space.

B HAL controls most of the functions of the spaceship, can talk like a human being and has human emotions. But David and Frank discover that HAL has made a serious mistake and secretly they discuss what to do.

C David leaves the spaceship to help his friend, but he is too late to save him. HAL then refuses to let David return to the spaceship, telling him that the mission is too important for David to put it in danger, and that he knows about their plans to disconnect him. But David manages to get back into the spaceship, and turns the computer off.

D A spaceship is on its way to the planet Jupiter to find out more about a strange rock which has been giving out signals suggesting evidence of intelligent life. While the other crew members are frozen in deep sleep for the long journey, David Bowman and Frank Poole are left to look after the spaceship with the help of a HAL 9000 computer, one of the most intelligent machines ever made.

E However, HAL sees their secret talks and realises that they're planning to disconnect him. So while Frank is outside the spaceship, HAL kills him.

11   🔲 Listen for main ideas. This is an extract from the book *2001: A Space Odyssey*; decide in which paragraph in 10 it happens.

12   Build your vocabulary. Read the passage again and make a list of words which you don't know, and another list of words which you recognise but still don't understand. Check your list with another student. Can he/she help you?

Now find three or four words from the passage which could go in each of the following categories

- the universe   - adventure
- life   - technology

Compare your words with another student.

13   Computers are used more and more in everyday life. They are also becoming more human. What can they replace? Think about:

- language learning   - medical care
- communications   - banking
- shopping   - newspapers

With your partner, choose one topic and tell others in the class how computers could change things in the future.

14   The interview with Arthur C. Clarke finishes with a discussion about living on other planets and the possibility of other forms of life in space. Before you listen, work in pairs and discuss your answers to the following questions.

1   Do you think people will ever live on other planets?
2   If so, which planets would we live on?
3   Would people want to live on another planet with a difficult climate and atmosphere?
4   Could we ever prove we were alone in the universe?
5   Do you think we would like to find other forms of life in space?

15   Read and predict. Arthur C. Clarke's replies are summarised below. Match them with the questions.

A   People can live happily anywhere they wish.
B   No, because the universe is so large that we can never be sure.
C   If we continue to live on Earth, eventually we'll live on other planets.
D   Yes, because in a big, cold universe, we'd like to think we're not alone.
E   The Moon and Mars.

🔲 Now listen and check.

16   Work in two groups.

> GROUP **A**
>
> **Would you like to live on another planet? Discuss the kind of life you would like to live there.**

> GROUP **B**
>
> **If you met someone from outer space, what would you do? Discuss what you would do to show the person something about life on Earth, and the questions you would ask about life on their planet.**

17 🔲 Listen to the end of the interview with Arthur C. Clarke. Find two things that he wants to do in the future.

18   Think of two things that you want to do in the future and discuss them with your partner.

> I want to . . .
> I'd like to . . .
> I hope to . . .

Pronunciation and Structure Review: page 164.

Unit 28 Making deductions

1 Build your vocabulary. Look at the photograph. Which of the following things can you see?

queue	boarding card
immigration control	hand luggage
duty-free shop	ticket
departure lounge	suitcase
check-in desk	customs
bookstall	passport
flight number	

2 Which of the following things do you expect to do at an airport *before* you board the plane?

check in	show your passport
get on	fasten your safety belt
change money	get off
go through customs	visit the duty-free shop
land	be delayed
take off	

3 Say what it looks as if the people are doing in the photograph.

Example: It looks as if the woman at the front of the queue is checking in.

4 Read and connect ideas. The sentences below come from two dialogues:

1 Confirming the reservation for a return flight by phone.
2 Checking in at the airport.

Decide which sentences belong to which dialogue.

- And could you tell me your flight number?
- Non-smoking by the window. Do you have any hand luggage?
- Ridley – that's R–I–D–L–E–Y.
- Yes, here you are.
- Smoking or non-smoking?
- Right, here's your boarding card. Have a nice flight.
- Yes, madam. What's your name, please?
- BA510 leaving on Sunday morning at 9.15.
- Non-smoking, please. A window seat if possible.
- Right, your flight is confirmed. Please check in at least an hour before departure.
- Good morning, sir. Can I see your ticket?
- Good morning, I'd like to confirm my flight back to Milan, please.
- Just my briefcase.

 **Listen and check.**

Write out the two dialogues. Then act out the dialogues in pairs.

5 Predict before listening.
Look at the photograph of
Robert and Annie. Say what it
looks as if they are doing.

6 ▣ **Listen and infer.**
Find out what has happened
and what Annie and Robert
are doing.

7 ▣ **Listen for specific**
information. Where has Robert
been recently?

A restaurant
B theatre
C taxi
D Annie's car
E shopping
F hotel room in Dundee
G Edinburgh Castle
H disco
I Annie's office
J bedroom
K friend's house

Now say what might have
happened.

Examples: He might have left it in the restaurant.
Someone might have taken it while he was out of the room.

8 Role play. Work in pairs within groups of four.

PAIR A

You are waiting at the airport in Terminal 1
for two friends coming from Paris on flight
AF 231. The plane landed an hour ago but
there is still no sign of them.

Go round the rest of the class and find out
what might have happened.

PAIR B

You have just arrived at the airport in
Terminal 2 from Paris on flight AF 231. But
your two friends are not there to meet you.

Go round the rest of the class and find out
what might have happened.

▣ **Listen to the announcement and find out what has happened.**
Greet your friends when you find them.

9 **Predict before reading. Work in pairs. Look at the picture and make deductions about what you see.**

Talk about:
- the place
- the country
- the season
- the people
- what they do
- what they're doing there

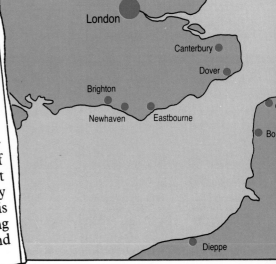

It looks as if . . .
He looks like a(n) . . .

Perhaps he's . . .
It's probably . . .

He $\begin{array}{l} \text{may} \\ \text{might} \\ \text{could} \end{array}$ be . . .

10 **Read for main ideas.**
Check whether you were right.

Saturday 25 June

Lost memory causes problem for police

An Englishman was arrested by police in a fishing village not far from Dieppe in France yesterday . . . and found to be suffering from a loss of memory. The police were called when the man, who spoke no French, refused to pay a bill of 82F for a large meal which he had just eaten. When the police searched him, they found no money on him at all. When an interpreter arrived, it became clear that the man couldn't remember either his name or how he got to the fishing village. His loss of memory is probably due to a head injury. At the police station the police found identity papers on him. Apparently he had left his home almost a week ago. They are now trying to discover how he got to France . . . and where his wallet is!

London

Canterbury

Dover

Brighton

Newhaven   Eastbourne

C

Boul

Dieppe

11   Work in groups.

GROUP **A**

Here are some of the things the French police found in the man's pockets when they searched him. Find out as much information about him as possible.

BRITISH RAIL

Brighton
to
Newhaven

Date **24 June**

BRIGHTON NOVELTIES LTD
2 Seaview Esplanade, Brighton, Sussex.

21 June

Dear Sir,
Thank you for your telephone call. Please come to our offices at the above address for an interview at 3pm on Thursday 23 June.

I'll see you as planned outside the London Astoria Theatre on Wednesday. But if you love me, I want you to promise never to see Jane again.

Trattoria La Rampa
3 Hyde Street, London

20 June **£9.50**

Tell Group B about what you have found out.

GROUP **B**

Here are some of the things the British police found when they searched the man's flat. Find out as much information about him as possible.

Representatives wanted
Phone Brighton 002891

ACME INSURANCE LTD
67 Hyde Street, London

Friday 17 June

Dear Mr Harrison,
We regret to inform you that we shall not be able to offer you any more work as from today. This is because of your

Jane 6 p.m. Thursday Brighton Pier

PASSPORT
UNITED KINGDOM OF GREAT BRITAIN AND NORTHERN IRELAND

Name of bearer *Henry Harrison*

National status *British*

Occupation *Insurance Salesman*

Address *3, Mallon St. London*

No. of passport

Tell Group A about what you have found out.

---

12   Work with people from other groups and discuss what might have happened.

	may		
He	might	have	...
	could		

Write a short report of what you know about the man and suggest what might have happened to him during the week.

13   Think about where you have been and what you have been doing during the last week. Make a list of things such as restaurant bills, tickets, etc. that you have received or used. You can invent the details if you like!

Now ask other students to say what you might have done, and where you could have been. Try to guess what they have been doing as well.

Pronunciation and Structure Review: page 165.

Expressing doubt and certainty

1   In Unit 26, Bill invited Jean to spend the day with him. Jean accepted the invitation. But it wasn't a very successful day. Look back at page 109 and say where they were supposed to go and what they were supposed to do.

Examples: They were supposed to leave early.
They were meant to be at the airport at six in the evening.

2   Predict before listening. Look at the photograph. Say what you think might have happened.

Examples: The car might have broken down.
They might have run out of petrol.

3   🔲 Listen and infer. Read the following statements. Then listen and decide if they are true or false.

1   They had a wonderful day.
2   They left early.
3   It was a sunny day.
4   Bill had lots of money.
5   They had nothing to eat at lunch.
6   Bill lost his temper.
7   Jean forgot her handbag.
8   The police towed Bill's car away.
9   They went to the beach.
10   Jean didn't go swimming.
11   They didn't get to the airport in time.
12   Bill telephoned the airport.

4   Work in pairs and check your answers. Explain your reasons.

Examples: They can't have had a wonderful day because everything went wrong.
They must have left late because Jean overslept.

5 Read and connect ideas. Look at the conversation between the people at the airport. Decide where these phrases should go.

- I'm sure they are.
- I'm sure they will.
- I'm sure they did.
- I'm sure we didn't.
- I'm sure it did.
- I'm sure we have.
- I'm sure they haven't.

PASSENGER 1:	I wonder where they are. The tour company must have told their representatives we were coming.
PASSENGER 2:	. . . They can't have forgotten.
PASSENGER 3:	. . .
PASSENGER 2:	We didn't take the wrong flight, did we?
PASSENGER 1:	. . . They looked at our tickets when we checked in, didn't they?
PASSENGER 3:	. . . And we've arrived at the right airport, haven't we?
PASSENGER 2:	. . . They're just late, that's all.
PASSENGER 1:	Yes, you're right. . . . I hope they get here soon.
PASSENGER 3:	. . .

▣▣ Now listen and check.

6 Read and predict. Complete the blanks in Jean and Bill's conversation with appropriate short responses. Use: *I'm sure . . . .*

BILL:	They must have arrived by now.
JEAN:	. . . Did head office tell you how many people there were?
BILL:	. . . but I can't remember.
JEAN:	I suppose they're waiting in the arrivals lounge.
BILL:	. . . I don't see what else they can do. They can't go anywhere, can they?
JEAN:	. . . Not until the coach arrives, anyway. It'll get there very soon, won't it?
BILL:	Yes, . . . And the driver will know what to do. He's very good.
JEAN:	. . . Bill, I've just thought of something. Can we ring the airport? They could make an announcement, couldn't they?
BILL:	You're right. . . . Let's look for a call box. Oh dear, this has never happened to me before.
JEAN:	. . .

▣▣ Listen and check.

7 Write a paragraph describing Jean and Bill's day out together. Say what was supposed to happen and what happened instead.

8 Work in pairs. Look at each cartoon, and think of one thing that must have happened and one thing that can't have happened.

9   Build your vocabulary. Which of the following sports can you see in the picture?

swimming   running   football   tennis   basketball   cycling
rugby   shooting   cricket   golf   sailing   riding

Which of the sports are *not* Olympic sports?

10   Read for main ideas. The passage on page 123 was written in 1986 when Barcelona was chosen to be the city to hold the Olympic Games in 1992. Read the passage and choose the best summary from the sentences below.

A   Barcelona has tried to organise the Olympic Games on many occasions, and as a result is well prepared for 1992.

B   Barcelona is a suitable place to hold the Olympic Games in 1992 because of its links with the Olympic Movement, the 500th anniversary of the discovery of America and the fact that all the facilities are nearly ready.

C   There are four areas in Barcelona where the Olympic Games will be held, all close to the city centre: Montjuïc for the athletics events; the Diagonal area for many of the preliminary events, including the football competition; Vall d'Hebron for cycling; and Parc de Mar for the Olympic Village.

BARCELONA—OLYMPIC CITY

The city of Barcelona has been linked with the Olympic Movement for many years. In 1920, it first offered to organise the games, and repeated its invitation in 1931 and 1966. The choice of Barcelona—Olympic city 1992—is a particularly good one. It is the 500th anniversary of Columbus's discovery of America, after which he sailed back to Barcelona.

The Olympic facilities are excellent. They are all within five kilometres of each other and are linked by good roads through the city. The Montjuïc area will hold up to eleven sports finals, and the Communications Media Centre is equipped to offer its services to 10,000 journalists. The Olympic Stadium, first built in 1929 for 80,000 spectators, is being rebuilt for field and track events. The Sports Palace has a capacity of 17,000 people and will hold the competitions in

gymnastics, swimming, volleyball, basketball and wrestling.

The Diagonal area is holding several preliminary competitions in the Barcelona Football Club stadium, which has a capacity of 120,000 spectators. There are also a number of first-class hotels in this area, as well as all the cultural facilities of the University of Barcelona.

The cycling races are taking place in the Vall d'Hebron area in a stadium built in 1984 for the World Cycling Championships. In Parc de Mar, facing the Mediterranean, work will begin very soon on the Olympic Village where the competitors stay. No less than three-quarters of the facilities needed to hold the Olympic Games in Barcelona are already built.

11   Say what Barcelona will and won't have to do to prepare for the Games.

Examples: The town won't have to build a stadium for the cycling events.
They'll have to build an Olympic Village.

12   Work in three groups.

GROUP A

You are on the Olympic Committee of Pierreville, one of three towns which may be chosen to hold the next Olympic Games. Pierreville is a large, polluted industrial city with a good airport but no big stadium. It has a large swimming pool and a sports centre.

GROUP B

You are on the Olympic Committee of Smithtown, one of three towns which may be chosen to hold the next Olympic Games. Smithtown is a small town in the mountains, very pretty and friendly but difficult to get to. You have no facilities except a huge football stadium.

GROUP C

You are on the Olympic Committee of Frankdorf, one of three towns which may be chosen to hold the next Olympic Games. Frankdorf is a medium-sized city with a stadium and a sports centre, and it is near an international airport. However, the facilities you will have to build will be quite a long way from the town centre.

Make a list of things which you will and won't have to do to prepare your town for the Olympic Games. Draw a map of your Olympic City.

13   Now present your proposals to the rest of the class and listen to other proposals.

Vote for the best town. (You cannot vote for your own town!)

Pronunciation and Structure Review: page 167.

Checking what you know

1 Work in pairs. Look at the photographs on the left and say what it looks as if David, Robert and Jean are doing.

2 Discuss what might have happened, must have happened or can't have happened since you last saw each character. Then write sentences giving your conclusions.

Examples: Robert must have packed his bags.
He might have called for a taxi . . .

3 📼 Listen for main ideas. Look at the list of things David has to do when he gets back. Then listen to the conversation. Which things has his secretary already done?

A Ring mother
B Edit Arthur C. Clarke recording
C Answer mail
D Finish report
E Go to bank
F Book studio for Thursday morning
G Plan new programmes
H Organise meeting to report on trip

Now say what David will have to do and what he won't have to do.

4 📼 Listen for main ideas. Listen to Robert's conversation and say what will happen if:

• the taxi doesn't come soon
• there's a lot of traffic
• he doesn't get to the station on time
• he misses his train to London
• he takes a train tomorrow

5 Make sentences using *Unless* . . .

Example: Unless the taxi comes soon, he'll be late.

6 📼 Listen for main ideas. What do you think Jean should do?

Leave and go home
Wait for Bill
Order dinner
Order dinner and let Bill pay
Telephone Bill to see if he's coming
Refuse to speak to him again
Find a new job

📼 Now listen to the rest of the conversation.

7 Work in groups. Discuss which of the following things Jean, Bill, Robert, Annie and David are likely or unlikely to do in the future.

• go to Canada
• get married
• change jobs
• miss the plane
• buy a (new) car

• return to Britain
• have (more) children
• produce TV programmes
• leave Barcelona
• become famous

Now choose three of the characters, and write short paragraphs about their future. Say what you think they are likely or unlikely to do.

8 Give your opinions on the statements below. Say if you think they are:

A Certain	D Not certain
B Likely/Probable	E Unlikely
C Possible	F Impossible

America will have a woman president.
A president will replace the Queen/King in Britain.
People will live longer in the future.
There will be a world war in our lifetime.
Everyone will have enough to eat.
People will live on the moon.
Computers will replace books.
Teachers will be better paid.
Cars won't be allowed in the cities.
Pollution of the seas and countryside will get worse.

If you do not agree with the statements, say what you think might happen.

9 Work in pairs.

> *STUDENT A*
>
> **Choose a unit in this book and write down five words which you can find in it. Show your list of words to your partner. He/She must guess which unit the words come from.**

> *STUDENT B*
>
> **Look at your partner's list of words taken from a unit in this book. Guess which unit the words come from. If you guess correctly, you score a point.**

Change round when you have finished. The first person to get five points is the winner.

10

CAN YOU . . . SPEAK ENGLISH?

PREPARATION

On five separate small pieces of card, write GREEN, RED, BLUE, PURPLE and YELLOW, or colour them. These are the colour cards. Work in groups of two to six people. Put all the cards in five piles according to their colours.

AIM OF THE GAME

To be the first player to reach the centre by answering CAN YOU . . . ? questions.

HOW TO PLAY

1 Each player places a counter in the centre.
2 Throw a dice in turn and move the number of spaces shown.
3 When you land on a colour square, the other players will choose a CAN YOU . . . ? question from the colour question box to ask you. They must choose a different question each time. They must also think of an extra question on the same subject to ask you. If the group decides you haven't answered the CAN YOU . . . ? question properly, you must wait a turn. If they can't think of an extra question to ask you, you can throw again.
4 You can look for help in the unit as long as your dice shows 2, 4 or 6. The unit number is shown next to the question.
5 If you land on a square marked !, you can throw the dice again.
6 If you land on a colour corner and answer the CAN YOU . . . ? question correctly, you get a colour card. When you have collected all five colour cards, throw the dice and move towards the centre.
7 The first player to reach the centre and answer a final question chosen from any colour question box is the winner.

Can you. . .
- say where you live, where you are from and what you do? (1)
- talk about your daily routine? (2)
- describe what your ideal man/woman looks like? (3)
- describe two exciting things you have done in your life? (4)
- say what you are going to do next week? (5)
- describe what your best friend is like? (1)
- describe the qualities you need to be a politician? (2)
- make nice comments about other people? (3)
- describe five important events in your life? (4)
- say what will happen if you learn to speak English? (5)

Can you . . .
- say what you like and don't like doing? (7)
- describe what makes you angry, bored and afraid? (8)
- say what you need to take on a visit to your country? (9)
- say what you were doing at this very moment a week ago? (10)
- complain about something? (11)
- invite someone to go somewhere this weekend? (7)
- react to good news about something? (8)
- say what you should and shouldn't do while driving in your country? (9)
- say what you were doing at midnight last New Year's Eve? (10)
- apologise for something you have done? (11)

Can you . . .
- describe how a house is built? (13)
- say what happened before and after you arrived at school today? (14)
- say what someone you know should or shouldn't have done this week? (15)
- say what your teacher told you to do for this activity? (16)
- say what you want to know about improving your English vocabulary? (17)
- describe a famous landmark in your country? (13)
- react with interest to something in the news this week? (14)
- give your opinion about your favourite sports person or team? (15)
- ask for permission to do something in the classroom? (16)
- say what you think twine, torpedo and dangle mean? (17)

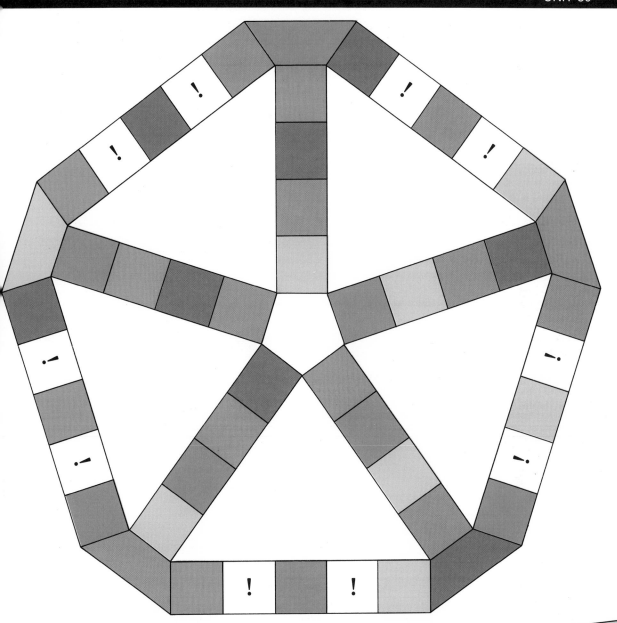

Can you . . .

- say what a *bottle opener*, *washing-up liquid* and *scissors* are for? (19)
- say what the best way to get from home to the town centre is? (20)
- say how a cassette player works? (21)
- describe three things you used to do as a child? (22)
- check the rules of this game using question tags? (23)
- describe in detail *a wallet*, *cheese* and a *bicycle*? (19)
- compare with someone how you both spend your weekends? (20)
- say what will happen if you leave school an hour later today? (21)
- describe three things about how life used to be in your country? (22)
- report the last thing the person on your right said? (23)

Can you . . .

- describe things that are certain, likely and unlikely to happen today? (25)
- suggest what you all can do to continue learning English? (26)
- say where you would live if you were very rich? (27)
- say what it looks as if the Queen and Mrs Thatcher are doing in the photograph on page 106? (25)
- describe three things you're supposed to do today? (29)
- describe three things that certainly won't happen by the year 2000? (25)
- make three promises? (26)
- describe three things which you would do if you weren't at school now? (27)
- say what might have happened at home today? (28)
- describe two things you will and won't have to do this week? (29)

127

Language Review

Unit 1   Talking about people

🔲 PRONUNCIATION

1.1   Listen and repeat

English   Irish   producer
charming   sensitive   apartment

How many syllables are there in each word?

1.2   How many syllables are there in each of these words?

company   seven   anxious
programme   serious   everyone

Read the words aloud. Then play the cassette and check. Listen and repeat. Mark the stressed syllables.

1.3   Listen and underline the words which are stressed.

Jackie is very hard-working – sometimes she works nine hours a day. She's always reliable and she never forgets anything. And she's very friendly . . . she's always pleasant to other people.

Write down the stressed words on a piece of paper. Close your book and use the stressed words to repeat what you've just heard.

STRUCTURE REVIEW

STRUCTURES

Look back at Unit 1 and complete the boxes.

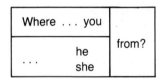

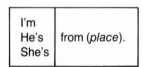

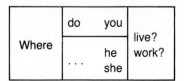

🔲 EXERCISES

Now play the cassette.

1.1   Ask for personal information.

Sheila's from Australia.
Where's Tom from?

Helen and Andy live in Glasgow.
Where do Mike and Janet live?

a)   Sheila/from Australia/Tom?
b)   Helen and Andy/live/Glasgow/Mike and Janet?
c)   Carlos/actor/Maria?
d)   Susie/works/shop/you?
e)   I/teacher/your husband?
f)   We/from Sweden/your friends?

I We They	live in work in/at	
He She	. . . in works in/at	(place).

| What | . . . you | do? |
| | does he she | |

| I'm He's She's | a(n) (job). |

1.2 Give personal information.

Where's Tom from?
He's from the USA.

Where do Mike and Janet live?
They live in Edinburgh.

a) Tom/from the USA
b) Mike and Janet/live/Edinburgh
c) Maria/dancer
d) you/work/hospital
e) your husband/salesman
f) your friends/from Denmark

| What's | he she | . . . ? |

| He's She looks | very quite/rather a little | sensitive. |
| He She | isn't doesn't . . . | at . . . shy. |

1.3 Talk about people's character.

Antonio is rather shy.
Really? He doesn't look at all shy.

a) Antonio/rather shy
b) Sally/very serious
c) Pedro/quite anxious
d) Mrs Carter/very kind
e) Mr Rogers/quite bad-tempered
f) Diana/a little selfish

| I | like don't like . . . mind | children. working. |

1.4 Say how these people feel about things.

How does David feel about swimming?
He likes swimming.

How does Jean feel about waiting in queues?
She doesn't mind waiting in queues.

a) David/swimming/likes
b) Jean/waiting in queues/doesn't mind
c) Robert/driving in town/doesn't like
d) David/getting up early/doesn't mind
e) Jean/football/doesn't like
f) Robert/flying/likes

1.5 Now say how you feel about the same things.

How do you feel about swimming?
I like swimming.   or
I don't mind swimming.   or
I don't like swimming.

Unit 2   Talking about work

📼 PRONUNCIATION

2.1   Listen and repeat.

/w/	/v/
wine	vine
wet	vet
west	vest
while	vile

Now listen and tick the words you hear.

2.2   Listen and write these words in the correct column.

we	were	verse	work
van	village	wear	very

/w/	/v/

Now read the words aloud.

2.3   Listen and underline the words which are stressed.

You need to be able to work in a team, and you have to be hard-working. It gets very busy here at lunchtimes – we don't stop running for three hours. And you can't sit down for a moment, and your feet hurt, and you're tired and hungry and you still have to be polite and charming to the customers.

Write down the stressed words on a piece of paper. Close your book and use the stressed words to repeat what you've just heard.

STRUCTURE REVIEW

STRUCTURES

Look back at Unit 2 and complete the boxes.

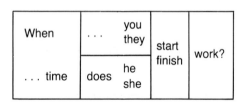

📼 EXERCISES

Now play the cassette.

2.1   Look at the chart. Say what time Jean and Robert do things.

What time does Jean get up?
She gets up at seven o'clock.

What time does Robert get up?
He gets up at a quarter past eight.

		Jean	Robert
a)	get up?	7 a.m.	8.15 a.m.
b)	have breakfast?	7.30 a.m.	8.45 a.m.
c)	start work?	8 a.m.	9.30 a.m.
d)	have lunch?	1.30 p.m.	1.30 p.m.
e)	finish work?	7 p.m.	5.30 p.m.
f)	go to bed?	11.30 p.m.	11.30 p.m.

2.2 **Ask what time David and his family do things.**

Ask when David gets up.
When does David get up?

a) David/get up?
b) his wife/start work?
c) she/have lunch?
d) the children/go to school?
e) David/finish work?
f) the children/go to bed?

	do	you	
. . . often	. . .	he	travel abroad?
		she	

Once		week.			day.
Twice	. . .	month.		Every	week.
Three . . .		year.			month.

2.3 **Say how often people do things.**

How often do the Pipers have a holiday?
They have a holiday twice a year.

a) the Pipers/have a holiday/twice/year
b) Robert/go to the dentist/every/six months
c) Jean/write to her mother/every/week
d) David and his wife/go to the theatre/once/month
e) Robert/play tennis/three times/week
f) Jean/go swimming/every/day

You			
He	must	be reliable.	
She			
		. . . able to drive.	
You	have . . .	know . . . to type.	
	need to		
He	. . . to	be good . . . using tools.	
She	needs to		

2.4 **Say what skills you need for the jobs.**

A doctor.
To be a doctor, you must be able to look after people.

a) doctor/must/be able/look after people
b) architect/need/be good at/design things
c) teacher/have/be patient
d) journalist/need/be good at/write stories
e) waiter/must/be polite
f) secretary/have/be able/type

Unit 3   Describing appearance

🎦 PRONUNCIATION

3.1   Listen and repeat.

/h/	Without /h/
hair	air
high	eye
hear	ear
hand	and

Now listen and tick the words you hear.

3.2   Listen and write these words in the correct column.

arm	heart	old	ill
height	how	he	is

/h/	Without /h/

Now read the words aloud.

3.3   Listen and underline the words which are stressed.

MAN: Hello. Can I help you?
WOMAN: Yes, are you Dr Smith?
MAN: No, I'm not.
WOMAN: Oh dear, I'm looking for Dr Smith. Have you seen him? He's tall, with grey hair and a moustache. He wears glasses.
MAN: No, I'm sorry. I haven't seen him.

Now listen and read aloud what the woman says.

STRUCTURE REVIEW

STRUCTURES

Look back at Unit 3 and complete the boxes.

	do	you	
What	does	he she	look . . . ?

🎦 EXERCISES

Now play the cassette.

3.1   Say what the people look like.

What does Annie look like?
She's tall, with curly auburn hair and blue eyes. She's about twenty.

a)   Annie/tall, curly auburn hair, blue eyes/20
b)   David/tall, slim, brown hair, blue eyes/40
c)   David's wife/short, slim, long dark hair, brown eyes/35
d)   Robert/average height, short brown hair, grey eyes/25
e)   Jean/tall, slim, blonde hair, blue eyes/23

I'm He's She's	(age/height/build) with (hair/eyes).

When I . . . young, I was	(much)	slimmer. fatter.
Now my hair is		shorter. longer.

3.2   Make comparisons.

When I was young, my hair was curly.
Now it's much straighter.

a)   my hair/curly/straight
b)   she/quite fat/slim
c)   he/very thin/fat
d)   I/short/tall
e)   her hair/long/short
f)   his hair/fair/dark

| What a(n) | extraordinary hat!
short skirt! |
| ... | beautiful flowers!
lovely hair! |

3.3 Make exclamations.

Tall man.
What a tall man!

a) tall man
b) extraordinary story
c) exciting news
d) lovely meal
e) terrible weather
f) interesting photographs

| He's
She's | got | such | a big nose!
long hair! |
| He's
She's | | ... | thin!
tall! |

3.4 Disagree with the statements.

It's such an exciting film!
I don't think it's so exciting.

a) exciting film
b) hard-working students
c) difficult exercise
d) pretty girl
e) friendly people
f) boring book

| He's
That's
She's | ... | man
one
woman | who ...
whose ... |

| He's
She's
They're | standing by the door.
laughing. |

3.5 Say who the people are.

Which is Dr Wilson?
He's the man who's wearing a white jacket.

a) Dr Wilson/man/wearing a white jacket
b) Mrs Mangano/woman/sitting on the sofa
c) Sylvia/girl/playing the piano
d) Roberto and Angela/ones/dancing
e) Mr Parker/man/smoking a cigar
f) Jack Mason/one/standing by the window

Unit 4 Describing background and experience

🔲 PRONUNCIATION

4.1 Listen and repeat.

When were you born?

Where do you come from?

When did you start learning English?

Have you ever seen a ghost?

Have you ever been to America?

Have you ever played cricket?

Now mark the intonation with arrows: ↘
or ↗

4.2 Listen and underline the words which are stressed.

Jean O'Hara was born on the fourteenth of August 1964 in Dublin. But her father died in April 1975 when she was nearly eleven. So in 1977 her mother decided to take Jean and her brother Patrick back to London, where her mother lived before she got married. Jean went to school there and had a very happy time. She left school when she was eighteen in 1982.

Write down the stressed words on a piece of paper. Close your book and use the stressed words to repeat what you've just heard.

STRUCTURE REVIEW

STRUCTURES	EXERCISES
Look back at Unit 4 and complete the boxes.	**Now play the cassette.**

STRUCTURES

Look back at Unit 4 and complete the boxes.

. . . did	you he she they	leave school? start working?

I You He She We They	left school started working	. . . 9th June. . . . May. in 1977. a year . . . . month. last week.

I You . . . They	've	already	found a flat. seen the museum. had dinner.
He She	's		

I You We They	haven't	been to the church visited the city	yet.
He She	. . .		

. . . you ever	climbed a mountain? been camping?

Yes,	I have. (very) often. . . . /twice/three times.
No,	I . . . never.

EXERCISES

Now play the cassette.

4.1 Say when things happened.

When did Jean arrive in Barcelona?
She arrived in Barcelona last week.

a) Jean/arrive in Barcelona/last week
b) Robert/leave university/in 1984
c) the journalist/interview David/in May
d) Annie/last see Robert/fifteen years ago
e) Bill/meet Jean/on 14th June

4.2 Say what you have or haven't done.

What about the cathedral?
Yes, we've already visited the cathedral.

What about a swim?
No, we haven't had a swim yet.

a) visit the cathedral ✔
b) have a swim ✘
c) see the market ✘
d) go to the museum ✔
e) walk through the park ✘
f) buy some postcards ✔

4.3 Ask people about their experiences.

Drive a lorry.
Have you ever driven a lorry?

a) drive a lorry?
b) play the guitar?
c) meet a famous person?
d) go to the USA?
e) fly in a helicopter?
f) practise yoga?

... long	have	you they	lived there?
	has	he she	

For ten years.
... 1986.

4.4 Ask how long.

Robert lives in Canada.
How long has he lived in Canada?

a) Robert/live in Canada?
b) Jean/know Bill?
c) David/work for the BBC?
d) Jean/be in Barcelona?
e) Annie/have a television?
f) David and Annette/be married?

4.5 Say how long.

How long has Robert lived in Canada?
Since 1972.

How long has Jean known Bill?
For a few days.

a) Robert/live in Canada/1972
b) Jean/know Bill/a few days
c) David/work for the BBC/1981
d) Jean/be in Barcelona/9th June
e) Annie/have a television/two weeks
f) David and Annette/be married/ten years

She was depressed He stayed at home They took a taxi	... it was raining.

It was raining, so	she was depressed. he stayed at home. they took a taxi.

4.6 Give the reasons.

Why did Robert take a tent?
Because he wanted to go camping.

a) Robert/take a tent/want to go camping
b) Jean/apply for the job/speak good Spanish
c) David/call a taxi/have a heavy tape recorder
d) Annie/go to the station/want to meet Robert
e) Bill/invite Jean for dinner/like her

4.7 Look at exercise 6, and explain the consequences.

Robert wanted to go camping . . .
. . . so he took a tent.

Unit 5 Planning ahead

🔲 PRONUNCIATION

5.1 How many syllables are there in each of these words?

photograph   interview   hotel
bicycle   grandparent   plantation
newspaper   university

Mark the stressed syllables. Then read the words aloud. Play the cassette and check. Listen and repeat.

5.2 Underline the stressed words in this dialogue.

DAVID: Are there any other arrangements for Monday, Sally?

SALLY: No, but on Tuesday, Pat would like to see you at nine a.m. in studio four.

DAVID: I can't – I'm going to the doctor then. I'll be free at ten though.

SALLY: OK, I'll tell her – ten o'clock Tuesday.

DAVID: Good. Anything else?

SALLY: There's a union meeting at midday on Wednesday. They're discussing working conditions.

DAVID: OK . . . union meeting at twelve.

SALLY: Oh, and Simon wants to see you on Friday – at three in the afternoon.

DAVID: Fine.

Now listen and check.
Then listen and read aloud what Sally says.

STRUCTURE REVIEW

STRUCTURES

Look back at Unit 5 and complete the boxes.

What	. . .	you they	doing	tonight? tomorrow? next week?
	is	he she		

I	'm	going to the cinema.
We They	. . .	working.
He . . .	's	having a holiday.

🔲 EXERCISES

Now play the cassette.

5.1 Talk about people's future arrangements.

Is David travelling to Singapore?
No, he's travelling to Sri Lanka.

a) David/travel to Singapore/Sri Lanka
b) Jean/have dinner with Bill next week/tonight
c) we/go to the concert this evening/tomorrow evening
d) the tourists/visit the cathedral this afternoon/the museum
e) Robert/fly home next week/next month
f) Annie/see the doctor tomorrow/dentist

What	are	you they	going . . . do	tonight? tomorrow? next year?
	is	he she		

I	'm		have dinner.
We They	're	going to	play football.
He She	. . .		go to university.

5.2 **Ask about people's plans and intentions.**

David wants to visit a tea plantation.
Is he going to visit a tea plantation?

a) David/visit a tea plantation
b) the police/catch the robber
c) I/learn to drive
d) Jean/move into a flat
e) the students/pass the exam
f) Robert/travel round Scotland

When As soon . . .	I leave school	. . . start work. I'll leave home.

5.3 **Say when people will do things.**

When's Pierre going to start work?
He'll start work when he leaves school.

When are Claudia and Marco going to get married?
They'll get married as soon as they find somewhere to live.

Use 'when' and 'as soon as' in turn.

a) Pierre/start work/leave school
b) Claudia and Marco/get married/find somewhere to live
c) Manuela/leave school/be sixteen
d) Boris/buy a car/pass his driving test
e) you/clean the windows/have time
f) the children/have supper/come home

If	you work hard	you'll pass	the exam.
. . .		you'll fail	

5.4 **Talk about conditions.**

Dario will go to university if he works hard.
He won't go to university unless he works hard.

a) Dario/go to university/work hard
b) They/come to the party/finish work in time
c) You/feel better/go to bed early
d) Liliana/go to New York/have enough money
e) I/phone you/change my plans
f) We/win the match/score another goal

Unit 7 Talking about present interests and past events

📼 PRONUNCIATION

7.1 Listen and underline the stressed words.

I love going to the theatre.
I like reading.
I enjoy playing football.
I'm not keen on dancing.
I don't like playing tennis.
I hate sightseeing.

Now read the sentences aloud.

7.2 Underline the stressed words in this dialogue.

FRANK: Why don't we go to a museum
tomorrow?
PAT: I'm afraid I don't really like going to
museums. I'd rather go to a rock concert.
FRANK: But there isn't anything worth going to
at the moment. How about going dancing?
PAT: That's a great idea. I'd love to.

Now listen and check.
**Listen again and mark the intonation with
arrows. Then listen and read aloud what Pat
says.**

STRUCTURE REVIEW

STRUCTURES

Look back at Unit 7 and complete the boxes.

I We They	love like enjoy don't like hate	travelling. reading.
He She	loves likes enjoys . . . like hates	

I'm We're They're He's She's	not keen . . . sightseeing.

📼 EXERCISES

Now play the cassette.

7.1 Talk about people's likes and dislikes.

Does Robert like playing tennis?
Yes, he loves playing tennis.

Does Annie like watching football?
No, she's not keen on watching football.

a) Robert/play tennis/love
b) Annie/watch football/be not keen on
c) David and Annette/go to the theatre/enjoy
d) Jean/stay in the hotel/not like
e) Robert/listen to music/hate
f) Bill/work in Barcelona/love

| How . . . | going to a concert? |
| Why don't we . . . you like to | play tennis? |

| . . . a good idea. |
| I'd love to. |
| All right. |

| I'd . . . | go to the cinema. play football. |

| I'm sorry, I'm afraid | I can't. I don't like playing tennis. |

| I You We They | 've | just | arrived. seen a film. been to a concert. |
| He She | 's | | |

7.2 Say what you'd rather do.

How about going to the theatre?
Well, I'd rather see a film.

a) go to the theatre/see a film
b) play chess/have a game of cards
c) listen to some jazz/hear some rock music
d) go by coach/take the train
e) eat a hamburger/have a pizza
f) go camping/stay in a hotel

7.3 Talk about what people have done recently.

Jean arrived in Barcelona last week.
Oh, so she's just arrived in Barcelona.

a) Jean/arrive in Barcelona/last week
b) David/leave the office/a few minutes ago
c) Jean and Bill/meet/a few days ago
d) Annie/phone Robert/five minutes ago
e) I/go to the hospital/this morning
f) Robert/write to his parents/last night

Unit 8   Saying how you feel

PRONUNCIATION

8.1 Listen to the endings and write the words in the correct column.

annoyed   excited   frightened   surprised
worried   depressed   amused   tired
/d/   /t/   /id/

Now read the words aloud.

8.2 Underline the stressed words in these expressions.

Oh, I am sorry.   That's great!
What a nuisance!   How marvellous!
What a surprise!   How awful!

Now listen and check. Mark the intonation with an arrow. Then say the expressions aloud.

8.3 Listen to these sentences and reply. Use the expressions in exercise 2. They are in the right order.

a) My mother's not very well.
b) I've lost my address book.
c) I saw Pete yesterday. I haven't seen him for years.
d) I'm getting married in June.
e) I've just won a million pounds.
f) My sister broke her leg while she was skiing.

STRUCTURE REVIEW

STRUCTURES

Look back at Unit 8 and complete the boxes.

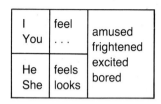

I You	feel . . .	amused frightened excited bored
He She	feels looks	

It . . . me feel	amused. frightened. excited. bored.

I We They	think	it's they're	amusing. frightening. exciting. boring.
He She	. . .		

Oh,	dear! I am sorry! really?

What . . .	nuisance! pity! surprise!

. . . That's	awful! marvellous nice! great!

EXERCISES

Now play the cassette.

8.1   Say how people feel.

Does David think wet weather is depressing?
Yes, it makes him feel depressed.

a)   David/wet weather/depressing?
b)   Annie/flying/exciting?
c)   old people/travelling/tiring?
d)   Robert/the story/amusing?
e)   Jean/the news/worrying?
f)   Bill/the loud music/annoying?

8.2   Talk about reactions.

Why do the children look amused?
Because they think the film is amusing.

a)   the children/amused/the film
b)   Jean/surprised/the announcement
c)   the crowd/excited/the tennis match
d)   the cat/frightened/the dog
e)   Robert/bored/the play
f)   the students/interested/the lesson

8.3   React to these situations.

I've lost my car keys.
Oh, what a nuisance!

a)   lost my car keys/nuisance!
b)   failed my driving test/pity!
c)   moved into a new flat/surprise!
d)   can't come to your party/pity!
e)   phone isn't working/nuisance!
f)   bought you a present/surprise!

Unit 9   Doing the right thing

🔲 PRONUNCIATION

9.1   Mark the stressed syllables in these words.

raincoat   credit   possible   temperature
dangerous   medicine   region   umbrella

Now listen and check. Then read the words aloud.

9.2   Decide which are the most important words in this dialogue and underline them.

DAVID: What do you think I should take, then?
HENRY: Well, when I was in Sri Lanka, the thing I needed most of all was a sun hat. It can get very hot. You should take some sun-cream as well. Are you going in the rainy season?
DAVID: I'm going in August.
HENRY: Then you'd better take an umbrella as well. And you ought to take a good insect spray. The mosquitoes can be very unpleasant, if not dangerous.

Now listen and check that these are the words which are stressed. Then listen and read aloud what Henry says.

STRUCTURE REVIEW

STRUCTURES

Look back at Unit 9 and complete the boxes.

I You He She We They	should(n't) ought(n't) . . .	wear a hat. take photos.

🔲 EXERCISES

Now play the cassette.

9.1   Give advice to a friend who is going to a wedding.

Do you think I should wear a blue shirt or a white one?
I think you should wear a white one.

Do you think I ought to take a raincoat or an umbrella?
I think you ought to take an umbrella.

Use 'should' and 'ought to' in turn.

a)   wear a blue shirt/a white one?
b)   take a raincoat/an umbrella?
c)   buy white shoes/black ones?
d)   give them some glasses/a picture?
e)   take it with me/send it by post?
f)   go by car/by train?

. . . better Don't forget to	take travellers' cheques.

9.2 Give advice in these situations.

Robert wants a train timetable.
He'd better go to the station.

a) Robert wants a train timetable/go to the station
b) We haven't got much bread left/buy some more
c) Annie has to get up very early/ask for an alarm call
d) David and Annette want to go to the theatre/book some tickets
e) You look very tired/go to bed early
f) Jean doesn't know how to get to the museum/look at a map

I You We They	(don't)	have . . .	to	wear a tie. take pills. leave a tip. take an umbrella.
He She	. . . needs			
	. . .	have need		

9.3 Say what isn't necessary.

I'm taking a day off work tomorrow.
I don't have to get up early.

Jean speaks fluent Spanish.
She doesn't need to have lessons.

Use 'have to' and 'need to' in turn.

a) I'm taking a day off work tomorrow/get up early
b) Jean speaks fluent Spanish/have lessons
c) Robert is travelling round Scotland with a tent/stay in hotels
d) We can walk to the cinema/take the car
e) Annie's got lots of food in the fridge/go to the supermarket
f) I'll give you some stamps/go to the post office

Unit 10 Talking about the past

 PRONUNCIATION

10.1 Listen and mark the stressed syllables.

accident motorway passenger overtake
police illegal ambulance pedestrian

Now read the words aloud.

10.2 Decide which are the most important words in the passage below and underline them.

A French burglar broke into a flat while the owners were away. While he was looking for things to steal, he found some cake in the kitchen, so he ate a piece. Then he found some beer and drank it. He was still feeling thirsty, so he drank a second can. He began to feel tired, so he sat on the sofa. Next evening when the owners got home he was still on the sofa, fast asleep. He woke up just before the police arrested him.

Now listen and check that these are the stressed words. Write down the stressed words on a piece of paper. Close your book and use the stressed words to repeat what you've just heard.

STRUCTURE REVIEW

STRUCTURES

Look back at Unit 10 and complete the boxes.

I He She	. . .	having lunch writing a report waiting for a bus	at 12.30.
We You . . .	were		

. . . he was	sightseeing, having lunch, shopping,	she was working.

While she was working, She was working . . .	the phone rang.

EXERCISES

Now play the cassette.

10.1 **Say what people were doing at eleven o'clock this morning.**

Annie.
Annie was typing a letter.

a) Annie/type a letter
b) Robert/visit an art gallery
c) Jean/talk to the hotel manager
d) The tourists/check in at reception
e) Bill/drive to the airport
f) The passengers/get off the plane
g) David/record a programme
h) David's wife/make a phone call
i) The teacher/drink a cup of coffee
j) The students/listen to the news

10.2 **Look at exercise 1, and say what people were doing at the same time.**

Annie and Robert.
While Annie was typing a letter, Robert was visiting an art gallery.

a) Annie/Robert
b) Jean/the tourists
c) Bill/the passengers
d) David/his wife
e) the teacher/the students

10.3 **Answer the questions using 'while'.**

Did the car break down?
Yes, the car broke down while we were driving onto the ferry.

a) car/break down/we/drive onto the ferry
b) you/find the keys/I/tidying the room
c) they/hear the news/they/watch TV
d) he/learn Japanese/he/teach in Tokyo
e) she/see the accident/she/standing at the bus stop

10.4 **Look at exercise 3, and answer the questions using 'when'.**

Did the car break down?
Yes, we were driving onto the ferry when the car broke down.

Unit 11   Facing the facts

📼 PRONUNCIATION

11.1 **Listen and tick the words which contain the sound /r/.**

party   restaurant   apparently   department
officer   friend   Irish   wrong

Now read the words aloud.

11.2 **Which of these words contain the sound /r/ ?**

reservation   manager   forget   replace
rope   terribly   sorry   receptionist

Now listen and check. Then read the words aloud.

11.3 **Listen and cross out any words in the written version which you don't hear.**

TELEPHONIST:	Good morning, Manley Stores. Can I help you?
CUSTOMER:	Yes, could I speak to someone in the clock department, please?
TELEPHONIST:	Hold the line, please.
ASSISTANT:	Good morning, this is the clock department. Can I help you?
CUSTOMER:	Yes, you can. I'd like to make a complaint about a new watch which I bought in your shop.
ASSISTANT:	What's wrong with it?
CUSTOMER:	It doesn't work. It's just stopped.
ASSISTANT:	How long have you had it?
CUSTOMER:	I bought it only a week ago. I've got the receipt here.
ASSISTANT:	Well, bring it back and we'll replace it for you.
CUSTOMER:	Thank you very much.

Now listen and read aloud what the customer says.

STRUCTURE REVIEW

STRUCTURES

Look back at Unit 11 and complete the boxes.

Could I speak	to (*person/department*)?
Could you ... me through	

Can I ...	a message?
Could you take	

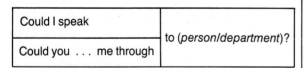

Can I ask him/her	to call	you	... ?
Could you ask him/her		me	

📼 EXERCISES

Now play the cassette.

11.1 **Make requests on the telephone.**

You want to leave a message.
Could I leave a message?

You want the telephonist to put you through to the manager.
Could you put me through to the manager?

Use 'Could I' and 'Could you' in turn.

a)   leave a message?
b)   put me through to the manager?
c)   speak to the doctor?
d)   take a message?
e)   phone back later?
f)   ask Jean to call me back?

Jean . . . Irish,	isn't she?
You speak Spanish,	don't . . . ?
They missed the plane,	. . . they?
Bill's . . . a car,	hasn't he?

11.2 **Show that you expect people to agree with you by adding question tags.**

Jean speaks Spanish.
Jean speaks Spanish, doesn't she?

a) Jean speaks Spanish.
b) Barcelona is a beautiful city.
c) Bill's been in Barcelona for a long time.
d) He was born in England.
e) Bill and Jean work for the same company.
f) You went to Spain last year.
g) We're going there this summer.
h) You can tell us where to stay.

I was waiting at the bus stop	. . . the accident happened.
I phoned for an ambulance	

11.3 **Say what was happening. Then say what happened.**

What was Annie doing when she smelt smoke?
She was reading in bed.

What did Annie do when she smelt smoke?
She phoned the fire brigade.

a) Annie/read in bed/smell smoke/phone the fire brigade
b) the robbers/leave the bank/hear the police car/start to run
c) the actor/make a speech/forget his words/walk off the stage
d) David/take photographs/hear a loud bang/drop his camera
e) Robert/run in the park/hurt his knee/sit on the grass
f) Jean and Bill/wait at the airport/hear the announcement/go to the information desk

Unit 13   Descriptbing processes and events

PRONUNCIATION

13.1 **How many syllables are there in these words?**

computers   cotton   manufacture   minerals
oranges   leather   diamonds   cameras

Now mark the stressed syllables and cross out the unstressed ones. Listen and check. Then read the words aloud.

13.2 **Underline the stressed words in this passage.**

Tea is made from the dried leaves of an evergreen plant which is called the Chinese Camellia. The green leaves are usually picked by hand, and then taken to the factory by truck. First the leaves are spread out on nylon shelves until they lose some of their moisture. Next the leaves are passed through rolling machines. The rolled leaves are then spread out again, this time on tables, and they turn brown as they absorb oxygen. After that, the leaves are dried in hot air and they turn black.

Now listen and check. Then read the passage aloud.

STRUCTURE REVIEW

STRUCTURES

Look back at Unit 13 and complete the boxes.

| Tea ... | grown
produced | in Sri Lanka. |

| The leaves ... | dried
spread out | on shelves. |

| Buddhism was founded ... a Hindu prince. |

| Temples ... built all over the island. |

 EXERCISES

Now play the cassette.

13.1 **Say where the products are from.**

Where is cotton grown?
Cotton is grown in Egypt.

a) Cotton/grow/Egypt
b) Coffee/produce/Kenya
c) Computers/manufacture/Japan
d) Leather goods/make/Italy
e) Iron/mine/Venezuela
f) Rubber/produce/India
g) Wheat/grow/Soviet Union
h) Paper/manufacture/Canada
i) Perfume/make/France

13.2 **Answer the general knowledge questions.**

Who invented the telephone?
It was invented by Alexander Graham Bell.

Who discovered the West Indies?
They were discovered by Christopher Columbus.

a) the telephone/invent/Alexander Graham Bell
b) the West Indies/discover/Christopher Columbus
c) the Sistine Chapel/paint/Michelangelo
d) *Rigoletto*/write/Verdi
e) the South Pole/first reach/Amundsen
f) the six *Brandenburg Concertos*/compose/Bach
g) Mount Everest/first climb/Tenzing and Hillary
h) the Pyramids/build/the Pharoahs

Unit 14   Telling a story

PRONUNCIATION

14.1 **Mark the intonation with an arrow to show interest and surprise.**

Don't you?   Didn't she?
Did you?   Weren't they?
Was it?   Do they?

Listen and check. Now read the questions aloud.

14.2 **Listen and react to these statements. Use the questions in exercise 1. They are in the right order.**

I don't believe in flying saucers.
But I'm sure I saw one last night.
It was just above my house.
My wife didn't believe me.
I called the police but they weren't interested.
Everyone just laughs at me.

14.3 Listen and put a ⅄ in the written versions when you hear some extra words.

An elephant escaped from a circus in Hamburg and knocked at a door with its trunk. The baker gave the elephant bread rolls. The owner described it as 'hungry'.

A girl who was angry with her friend decided to make him pay. When he went away for the weekend, she visited his flat and made a call.

The man returned and found the phone off the hook. He picked up the phone. He was connected to the speaking clock in York.

Listen again and write in the missing words. Choose from these words:

surprised harmless baker's fresh but yesterday elephant's home and phone boy listened New unlucky London

Now read the completed passages aloud.

STRUCTURE REVIEW

STRUCTURES

Look back at Unit 14 and complete the boxes.

He met a man	who had seen a ghost.
He talked to a lady	. . . son was living in Paris.
He found a hotel	where he could stay the night.
There's a room	. . . no one has been able to find.

I saw a ghost once.	. . . you?
He doesn't like chips.	Doesn't . . . ?
You've passed the exam.	Have I?
The film . . . very good.	Isn't it?

 EXERCISES

Now play the cassette.

14.1 Join the sentences with 'who', 'whose', 'which', or 'where'.

Robert has a cousin. She lives in Edinburgh.
Robert has a cousin who lives in Edinburgh.

a) Robert has a cousin. She lives in Edinburgh.
b) Edinburgh is the city. Robert was born there.
c) That's the bus. It goes to the station.
d) David has a friend. The friend knows Sri Lanka well.
e) Mr Davis is the man. His passport is missing.
f) We stopped at a café. We had lunch there.

14.2 Ask short questions.

Robert left Scotland fifteen years ago.
Did he?

Jean doesn't like ice cream.
Doesn't she?

a) Robert left Scotland fifteen years ago.
b) Jean doesn't like ice cream.
c) Annie hasn't come home yet.
d) David's children both speak French.
e) I can't swim.
f) They're going to Australia next week.
g) The restaurant isn't very expensive.
h) I've got tickets for the concert.

He paid his bill	and (then) he left before he left . . . leaving	the hotel.

He left the hotel	after paying after he . . . paid	his bill.

14.3 Say when people did things, using the past perfect tense.

When did Jean go to Spain?
After she'd worked in London.

a) Jean/go to Spain/work in London
b) the tourists/have lunch/visit the museum
c) Robert and Annie/have a drink/go to the cinema
d) Bill/go to the office/return from the airport
e) David/have dinner/unpack
f) Annie/phone her mother/have a cup of tea

14.4 Look at exercise 3 again. Say when people did things, using 'after' + —ing.

When did Jean go to Spain?
She went to Spain after working in London.

Unit 15   Saying what you think

PRONUNCIATION

15.1 Listen and mark the stress on these words.

amusing   ugly   extraordinary
exciting   frightening   disgusting
colourful   interesting

Which words are stressed on the first syllable?
Read them aloud.
Which words are stressed on the second syllable? Read them aloud.

15.2 Mark the stress on these words.

shocking   imaginative   amazing   beautiful
grotesque   fantastic   terrible   depressing

Which words are stressed on the first syllable?
Read them aloud.
Which words are stressed on the second syllable? Read them aloud.
Now listen and check.

15.3 The missing words in this passage are the stressed words. Fill in the blanks with these words.

century   styles   studied   region   wide
famous   Picasso   returned   works   Barcelona

The most . . . painter of this . . . is probably
. . . . He . . . in . . . and often . . . to this . . . of
Spain. His . . . cover a . . . range of . . . .

Now listen and check.
Then read the complete passage aloud.

STRUCTURE REVIEW

STRUCTURES

Look back at Unit 15 and complete the boxes.

I think	it's they're	shocking. amazing.

I You He She We They	should shouldn't	. . .	told the police. opened the door. gone to the party. read the letter.

. . .	did . . .	I you he she we . . .	tell the police? open the door? go to the party? read the letter?

📼 EXERCISES

Now play the cassette.

15.1 Say what you think.

What do you think of this painting?
I think it's very colourful.

a) painting/very colourful
b) shoes/rather ugly
c) building/extraordinary
d) play/rather depressing
e) photographs/quite interesting
f) newspaper/shocking

15.2 Say what people should or shouldn't have done.

Bill didn't reserve a table.
He should have reserved a table.

You parked outside the police station.
You shouldn't have parked outside the police station.

a) Bill didn't reserve a table.
b) You parked outside the police station.
c) Jean didn't look at the map.
d) We left the window open.
e) The students didn't do their homework.
f) I lost the phone number.

15.3 Look at exercise 2 again. Criticise people by asking questions.

Bill didn't reserve a table.
Why didn't he reserve a table?

You parked outside the police station.
Why did you park outside the police station?

Unit 16   Persuading people to do things

▣ PRONUNCIATION

16.1 Listen and underline the stressed words in this dialogue. Then mark the intonation with arrows.

WOMAN: Do you mind if I leave work early tonight?
MAN: I'd rather you didn't.
WOMAN: Oh, please! I need to go to the dentist.
MAN: Oh, all right then – but this is the last time.

Now listen and read aloud what the man says.

16.2 Underline the stressed words in this dialogue. Then mark the intonation with arrows.

MAN: Can I make a phone call, please?
WOMAN: No, I'm afraid you can't.
MAN: Look, I only want to call a taxi.
WOMAN: I'm sorry, but you aren't allowed to use this phone. There's a phone box outside.

Now listen and check. Then listen and read aloud what the woman says.

STRUCTURE REVIEW

STRUCTURES

Look back at Unit 16 and complete the boxes.

You'd better If I . . . you, I'd You should You . . . to	drive carefully. take an umbrella.

You'd better . . . If I were you, I . . . You shouldn't You oughtn't to	break the window. go to bed late.

▣ EXERCISES

Now play the cassette.

16.1 Give people advice.

I've got a job interview tomorrow.
If I were you, I'd wear a suit.

a) job interview tomorrow/wear a suit
b) headache/take an aspirin
c) should take more exercise/cycle to work
d) remember the telephone number/write it down
e) coffee-maker doesn't work/take it back to the shop
f) want to write a book/learn to type

16.2 Give people warnings.

It's the last train.
You'd better not miss it.

This water isn't clean.
If I were you, I wouldn't drink it.

Use 'You'd better not' and 'If I were you' in turn.

a) it's the last train/miss
b) this water isn't clean/drink
c) it's an important meeting/forget
d) this meat tastes bad/eat
e) it's a personal letter/read
f) the hair-drier isn't safe/use

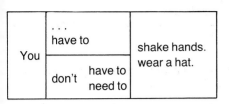

You	have to	shake hands.
	...	wear a hat.
	don't	have to
		need to

You mustn't	
You can't	take photographs.
You aren't ... to	

| He | told | her | (not) ... | shake hands. |
| She | | him | | take photographs. |

Do you ... if I sit down?	
May	
Can	I open the window?
...	

| Not at all – go ahead. |
| Yes, you can. |
| Yes, of course. |
| Oh, all right then. |

| I'd ... you didn't. |
| No, I'm afraid you .... |
| I'm ... , but you aren't allowed to. |

16.3 Report the instructions.

You must drive slowly.
She told me to drive slowly.

You can't stop on the motorway.
She told me not to stop on the motorway.

a) must drive slowly
b) can't stop on the motorway
c) have to wear a seatbelt
d) mustn't park outside the station
e) aren't allowed to cycle on the motorway
f) must drive on the left

16.4 Ask people if you may do things.

You want to turn on the television.
Do you mind if I turn on the television?

a) turn on the television?
b) make a phone call?
c) take off my shoes?
d) have a shower?
e) do some washing?
f) go to bed?

Unit 17   Speculating

🔘 PRONUNCIATION

17.1 Each question below has the same reply, but the stressed word is different each time. In each reply, underline the word which you think will be stressed.

a) Is Loch Ness seven kilometres west of Inverness?
No, Loch Ness is seven miles west of Inverness.

b) Is Loch Ness seven miles west of Edinburgh?
No, Loch Ness is seven miles west of Inverness.

c) Is Loch Long seven miles west of Inverness?
No, Loch Ness is seven miles west of Inverness.

d) Is Loch Ness seven miles east of Inverness?
No, Loch Ness is seven miles west of Inverness.

e) Is Loch Ness eleven miles west of Inverness?
No, Loch Ness is seven miles west of Inverness.

Now listen and check. Then work in pairs and read the questions and answers aloud.

17.2 Listen and correct all the statements with this sentence:

No, Loch Ness is supposed to be the home of the famous monster.

The sentence is the same, but the stressed word or words is different each time.

a) Loch Ness is the home of the famous monster.

b) Loch Long is supposed to be the home of the famous monster.

c) Inverness is supposed to be the home of the famous monster.

d) Loch Ness is supposed to be the home of the dangerous monster.

e) Loch Ness is supposed to be the home of the famous wild animal.

STRUCTURE REVIEW

STRUCTURES

Look back at Unit 17 and complete the boxes.

Can you tell me Do you know Have you . . . idea	where the station is? . . . the next train leaves? what time it arrives? how . . . it takes? if there's a hotel near here?

I don't know . . . like to know I wonder	where the station is. when the next train leaves. what time it arrives. how long it takes. if there's a hotel near here.

🔘 EXERCISES

Now play the cassette.

17.1 Make indirect questions.

What's the time? Have you any idea?
Have you any idea what the time is?

a) What's the time? Have you any idea?
b) Where's the theatre? Can you tell me?
c) How much are the tickets? I'd like to know.
d) When does the play start? Do you know?
e) Is it good? Have you any idea?
f) What's it about? I don't know.
g) Who are the actors? Do you know?
h) Will I enjoy it? I wonder.

. . .	's definitely (not) an animal in the lake.
It	may be an animal.

Perhaps I (don't) think I'm not sure	there's an animal in the lake. . . . a monster.

He She	must . . .	. . . a doctor. live in Canada.

17.2 Draw conclusions.

Jean isn't in the office.
She must be at the hotel.

Robert is camping in the rain.
He can't be very comfortable.

a) Jean isn't in the office/be at the hotel
b) Robert is camping in the rain/be very comfortable
c) Annie had no sleep last night/feel very tired
d) Mr Renshaw has lost his travellers' cheques/have much money
e) David works for BBC Radio 4/know my husband
f) Bill doesn't want anything to eat/be very hungry

Unit 19   Describing things

PRONUNCIATION

19.1 Listen to these sentences and mark the intonation with arrows.

a) It's a small square red clock with a white face.
b) I like the blue checked cotton shirt with short sleeves.
c) It's a large rectangular black leather bag with a shoulder strap.
d) It's a long grey woollen man's coat with a big collar.

Now read the sentences aloud.

19.2 Mark the intonation with arrows.

a) He's a tall fair-haired well-dressed Swede with a moustache.
b) She's wearing a white cotton shirt with long sleeves.
c) I've got a beautiful red Italian sports car with five gears.
d) It's a long interesting and amusing story with a strange ending.

Now listen and check.
Then read the sentences aloud.

19.3 Some of the words in the written version of this dialogue have been changed. Listen and correct any words which are different from what you hear.

JEAN: Well, I think that's just about everything.
BILL: How am I going to buy something for dinner?
JEAN: What are you going to make?
BILL: Ah, that's a secret. Make it and see.
JEAN: Really? Well, what's it made with?
BILL: Oh, just two tomatoes, one potato and onions, and a little celery . . . and parsley. . .
JEAN: There's a vegetable shop round the corner from my flat.
BILL: And I need a little jam, and little nice wine . . .
JEAN: That's easy . . .
BILL: And ridiculous, I promise. It's my speciality.
JEAN: I can't wait.

Now listen and read aloud what Bill says in your corrected version.

STRUCTURE REVIEW

STRUCTURES	📼 EXERCISES
Look back at Unit 19 and complete the boxes.	Now play the cassette.

He She	needs	a kettle. . . . scissors.
	doesn't need	a tin opener. . . . knives.

How	much	salt oil	. . .	there?	There's	. . . . a lot.
	. . .	eggs onions	are		There are	a few. . . . .

19.1 Ask questions about the recipe ingredients.

I need some pepper.
How much pepper do you need?

I need some tomatoes.
How many tomatoes do you need?

a) pepper? e) onions?
b) tomatoes? f) vinegar?
c) eggs? g) oil?
d) garlic? h) olives?

What	size shape colour	is it?

. . .	big heavy long	is it?

Where's it from?

What's it made . . . ?

19.2 Ask questions about a mystery object.

Is it round or square?
What shape is it?

Is it large or small?
How big is it?

a) round or square?
b) large or small?
c) red or blue?
d) weigh a lot?
e) French or Italian?
f) metal or plastic?

What's it for?

A kettle is		boiling water in.
A glass is		. . . out of.
Scissors are	. . .	cutting . . . .
A plate is		eating off.

19.3 Say what things are for.

What's a corkscrew for?
It's for opening bottles with.

a) corkscrew/open bottles with
b) knife/cut with
c) kettle/boil water in
d) cup/drink out of
e) soap/wash with
f) plate/eat off

It's	at the top at the bottom in the corner . . . the right on the left in the middle . . . the top right-hand corner in the bottom . . . corner	(of the . . .).

It's	on under behind in front . . . near next . . . between opposite	the . . . .

19.4 **Before you do this exercise, look at the painting called *Breakfast* on page 83. Say where people and things are in the painting.**

Where's the man?
He's on the right of the painting.

Where's the maid?
She's between the man and the woman.

a) man/right/painting
b) maid/between/man and woman
c) teapot/middle/table
d) cigar box/corner/painting
e) window/behind/woman
f) plant/in front/window

Unit 20   Making comparisons

🎜 PRONUNCIATION

20.1 **How many syllables are there in these words? Mark the stressed syllables and cross out the unstressed ones.**

factory   housing   entertainment   expensive
alcohol   tobacco   education   household
comfortable   station

Now say the words aloud.
Then listen and check.

20.2 **Listen and put a ʌ in the written version when you hear some extra words.**

ANNOUNCER: And now consumer affairs. The Consumer Council has issued a report on how we spend our money, and Dr Priscilla Watts is in the studio to tell us about it. Dr Watts, what do we spend our money on?

DR WATTS: Well, the biggest expense for the household is transport.
ANNOUNCER: That includes cars as well as trains and buses.
DR WATTS: Yes – and we spend 17% of our budget on transport. Close behind is housing – that includes rent and mortgage repayments.
ANNOUNCER: So we spend the same on housing as on food?
DR WATTS: Right.

Listen again and write in the missing words. Choose from these words; some of them can be used more than once:

here   about   just   of   to   private   course
do   Research   at   most   Britain   food   in
15%   and   we   average   That's

Now listen and read aloud what Dr Watts says in your completed version.

STRUCTURE REVIEW

STRUCTURES

Look back at Unit 20 and complete the boxes.

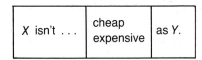

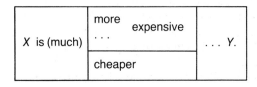

X is the	... expensive	form of transport.
	least	
	cheapest	

He spends more time sleeping	...	I do.
They start school later		we do.

EXERCISES

Now play the cassette.

20.1 Make comparisons.

Is Rio larger than São Paulo?
No, Rio isn't as large as São Paulo.

a) Rio/large/São Paulo
b) Paris/expensive/Copenhagen
c) film/good/book
d) Jean/old/Bill
e) train journey/interesting/coach journey
f) London/noisy/New York

20.2 Make comparisons.

Annie is quite young, isn't she?
Yes, she's younger than Robert.

The red shoes are quite expensive, aren't they?
Yes, they're more expensive than the black ones.

a) Annie/young/Robert
b) red shoes/expensive/black ones
c) Madrid/hot/Barcelona
d) coach/comfortable/bus
e) flying/safe/driving
f) trousers/cheap/jeans

20.3 Make comparisons.

David likes jazz, doesn't he?
Yes, he likes jazz more than Annette does.

a) David/like jazz/Annette
b) Annie/work hard/Robert
c) Bill/spend time cooking/Jean
d) the Spanish/have dinner late/the Norwegians
e) Bill/drive fast/Jean
f) the French/spend money on food/the British

He sleeps for 10 hours	but	I sleep for 7 hours.
They start at 9 a.m.	. . .	we start at eight.

20.4 **Join these sentences to express contrast.**

Jean likes coffee. Bill likes tea.
Jean likes coffee, but Bill likes tea.

Annie gets up at 7.30. Robert gets up at 8.15.
Annie gets up at 7.30, whereas Robert gets up at 8.15.

Use 'but' and 'whereas' in turn.

a) Jean likes coffee. Bill likes tea.
b) Annie gets up at 7.30. Robert gets up at 8.15.
c) I start work at 8. You start work at 9.
d) The train takes two hours. The coach takes five hours.
e) The Swiss watch costs £50. The Japanese one costs £10.
f) Jean has blonde hair. Her brother has dark hair.

Unit 21   Explaining how things work

PRONUNCIATION

21.1 **Underline the most important words in this passage and cross out the other words.**

First of all, plug in the machine and turn on the electricity. Then open the filter holder and place a filter paper inside. Put a teaspoon of coffee per cup in the filter paper and close the filter holder. Fill the coffee pot with water and pour it into the top of the machine. When you've put the pot under the filter again, press the switch at the bottom. As soon as the red light goes on, the water starts to heat up. After about five minutes, as soon as the bubbling noise stops, pour the coffee or leave it on the hotplate until you're ready.

Now listen and check if the words you underlined are stressed. Then read the passage aloud.

21.2 **Here are the stressed words taken from some instructions on how to use a cassette recorder. Decide what the rest of the instructions will say.**

Plug in.......machine......turn on ....electricity. Open.......front....... cassette recorder.......place.......cassette inside. Press.......button.......top.......machine ....cassette.......start.......play.

Now listen and check.
Then use the stressed words to repeat what you've just heard.

STRUCTURE REVIEW

STRUCTURES

Look back at Unit 21 and complete the boxes.

| Plug in the machine. |
| Turn on the electricity. |
| Take out the dishes. |

| When
. . . soon as | it | stops,
. . . stopped, | open the door. |

| If | the electricity isn't on,
you . . . close the door, | the machine
won't work. |

| Sharks are attracted
by light things, | . . . | wear dark clothing.
cover your arms and legs. |

| Wear dark clothing
Cover your arms and legs | because sharks are attracted
by light things. |

EXERCISES

Now play the cassette.

21.1 Give instructions on how to view a film on video.

What do I do when I've turned on the TV?
When you've turned on the TV, switch on the video recorder.

a) turn on TV/switch on video recorder
b) switch on video recorder/put in cassette
c) put in cassette/select video channel
d) select video channel/press PLAY button
e) press PLAY button/sit back and enjoy film

21.2 Say what will or won't happen.

What if I press the red button?
If you press the red button, the light will go on.

What if I don't switch on the video?
If you don't switch on the video, the machine won't work.

a) press red button/light go on
b) not switch on video/machine not work
c) open door/water pour out
d) turn black button/music get louder
e) turn off gas/food not cook
f) press PAUSE button/tape stop

21.3 Give advice with reasons.

Should I take an umbrella?
Yes, take an umbrella because it's the rainy season.

a) take umbrella/rainy season
b) drink bottled water/tapwater not safe
c) wear hat/sun very hot
d) drive slowly/roads not very good
e) pack some warm clothes/cold at night

21.4 Look at exercise 3, and give advice in a different way.

It's the rainy season, isn't it?
Yes, it is, so take an umbrella.

The tapwater isn't safe, is it?
No, it isn't, so drink bottled water.

Unit 22   Describing changes

🔊 PRONUNCIATION

22.1 Listen and underline four stressed words in each of these sentences.

a) She used to have long hair, but his hair used to be very short.

b) He used to live in the country, whereas she used to live in the town.

c) He used to have a huge garden, but her garden was tiny.

d) He used to go abroad for the summer, while she used to go to the seaside.

Now read the sentences aloud.

22.2 Underline the most important words in this dialogue and cross out the other words.

JEAN: Do you remember the other day, we were talking about what we used to do as children?

BILL: Yes, I remember. Why?

JEAN: Well, I've found a photo taken when I was twelve years old.

BILL: Oh, can I see?

JEAN: Yes, hang on a minute. It's here somewhere.

BILL: Did you use to have short hair?

JEAN: No, very long hair. And it used to be straight.

BILL: And what kind of clothes did you wear?

JEAN: Mostly jeans and sweat shirts. I didn't like wearing school uniform. Actually, I really wanted to be a boy.

Now listen and check if the words you underlined are stressed.

Then listen and read aloud what Bill says.

STRUCTURE REVIEW

STRUCTURES

Look back at Unit 22 and complete the boxes.

. . .	you he she they	use . . .	have long hair? wear jeans?

I He She We They	used didn't . . .	to	have short hair. wear jeans.

🔊 EXERCISES

Now play the cassette.

22.1   Ask Robert questions about his childhood.

Ask if he used to live in Canada.
Did you use to live in Canada?

Ask where he used to live.
Where did you use to live?

a)   live in Canada?
b)   where/live?
c)   where/go to school?
d)   like school?
e)   where/spend your holidays?
f)   what/do in your free time?

22.2   Talk about the lives of these people.

Has Annie always had shoulder-length hair?
No, she used to have short hair.

a)   Annie/shoulder-length hair/short hair
b)   Robert's parents/live in Canada/Scotland
c)   David/be a radio producer/an English teacher
d)   Jean/work in Barcelona/London
e)   the students/work so hard/be quite lazy
f)   Bill/live in the city/the country

People didn't use to travel much,	but whereas . . .	today they travel a lot.

Lots of families used to have servants	but they	don't	. . . . . .
Families used to be quite large		aren't	

22.3 Say how things have changed.

Does Robert smoke?
He used to smoke, but he doesn't any more.

a) Robert/smoke?
b) Jean/a waitress?
c) the Pipers/live in Brazil?
d) Annie/a cat?
e) the hotel/cheap?
f) the children/shy?

Unit 23 Finding things out

PRONUNCIATION

23.1 Listen and mark the intonation on the question tags with an arrow.

It's a nice day, isn't it?

It won't take long, will it?

You've done some shopping, haven't you?

There are so many people, aren't there?

I can go now, can't I?

She spoke very clearly, didn't she?

Now read the sentences aloud.

23.2 Here are the stressed words taken from a passage. Decide what the rest of the passage will say.

Another example.......first kind.......mystery.......happened.......Canada.......1790.......afternoon.......suddenly.......sun went in.......dark.......two days. Everyone thought.......end.......world.......But.......someone.......more scientific mind.......didn't believe.......after.......research......discovered.......caused.......fires.......New York.......places.

Now listen and check. Then use the stressed words to repeat what you've just heard.

STRUCTURE REVIEW

STRUCTURES

Look back at Unit 23 and complete the boxes.

It's 40 miles,	isn't . . . ?
He knew the number,	. . . he?
It . . . take long,	should it?
She hasn't lost the map,	. . . she?

EXERCISES

Now play the cassette.

23.1 Check the information by adding question tags.

Sri Lanka is an island.
Sri Lanka is an island, isn't it?

David hasn't been there before.
David hasn't been there before, has he?

a) Sri Lanka is an island.
b) David hasn't been there before.
c) Jean and Bill met in Barcelona.
d) Robert and Annie are cousins.
e) You aren't married.
f) They'll be careful.
g) David should reconfirm his flight.
h) The train wasn't late.

Direct speech
"It's about fifty miles," she said.
"We're going to be late," he said.
"I haven't booked a room," she said.
"I tried to phone," he said.
"It will take three hours," she said.

Indirect speech
She said it was about fifty miles.
He said they . . . going to be late.
She said she hadn't booked a room.
He said . . . had tried to phone.
She said it . . . take three hours.

Can you . . . me
Do you know
. . . you any idea

. . . you live?
when you arrived?
. . . happened?
who is he?
. . . long it will take?
why he slowed down?

23.2 Report what these people say.

WOMAN: It's not far to the airport.
She said it wasn't far to the airport.

MAN: I'm going to take a taxi.
He said he was going to take a taxi.

a) WOMAN: It's not far to the airport.
b) MAN: I'm going to take a taxi.
c) WOMAN: I'll drive you there.
d) MAN: I've already phoned for a taxi.
e) WOMAN: You look worried.
f) MAN: I don't know where I put my ticket!

23.3 Ask for information.

What's the flight number? Can you tell me?
Can you tell me what the flight number is?

a) What's the flight number? Can you tell me?
b) Where is the information desk? Do you know?
c) How long is the flight? Have you any idea?
d) When do we arrive in Taiwan? I want to know.
e) Which hotel are we staying in? I don't know.
f) Why is there a delay? I wonder.

Unit 25   Talking about the future (1)

🔊 PRONUNCIATION

25.1 Listen and repeat.

government   minister   conservative   socialist
election   president   parliament   cabinet

How many syllables are there in each of these words? Mark the stressed syllables and cross out the unstressed ones. Then say the words aloud.

25.2 How many syllables are there in these words? Read the words aloud.

political   representative   general   politician
authority   liberal   democrat opinion

Now listen and repeat.

25.3 Mark the woman's intonation with an arrow.

MAN: I think there'll be a woman president in the USA soon.
WOMAN: Do you? I think so too.
MAN: And she'll be elected within the next ten years.
WOMAN: Oh, no. No, it won't be as soon as that!
MAN: But there are some very good women politicians. I don't think it'll be long, you know.
WOMAN: Oh yes, it will! These things take time, you know.

Now listen and check. Then listen and read aloud what the woman says.

STRUCTURE REVIEW

STRUCTURES	EXERCISES

STRUCTURES

Look back at Unit 25 and complete the boxes.

will certainly	=	is/are . . . to
will . . .	=	is/are likely to
will possibly	=	may/ . . . /could
probably . . .	=	is/are unlikely to
certainly won't		

If	power stations
	  continue to burn coal,
	the government
	  does nothing,
		acid rain . . .
		increase.

Unless	power stations
	  stop burning coal,
	the government
	  does something,	

 EXERCISES

Now play the cassette.

25.1 Agree with the predictions.

It's certain to rain this afternoon.
Yes, it'll certainly rain this afternoon.

Annie and Robert are unlikely to play tennis.
No, they probably won't play tennis.

a) It's certain to rain this afternoon/will certainly
b) Annie and Robert are unlikely to play tennis/probably won't
c) Annie is likely to go shopping/will probably
d) Robert might go to a museum/will possibly
e) I'm certain they won't stay at home/certainly won't

25.2 Talk about future possibilities.

Will the police arrest the driver?
Yes, they'll arrest the driver if they catch him.

a) the police/arrest the driver/catch him
b) your sister/go to university/pass her exams
c) David/come to the meeting/have time
d) Jean and Bill/go to the concert/get tickets
e) Annie/buy a car/learn to drive
f) Robert/get married/fall in love

Unit 26   Talking about the future (2)

 PRONUNCIATION

26.1 Mark the intonation with an arrow.

I'll buy a newspaper for you, shall I?
Shall I do some shopping while I'm out?
How about going to the cinema tonight?
Why don't we go away for the weekend?
Let's turn on the television, shall we?
What about spending August in France?

Now read the questions aloud.
Listen and check. Then listen and repeat.

26.2 Listen and cross out any words in the written version which you don't hear.

BILL: Hello, Jean. How did you get on?
JEAN: Oh dear, not very well, I'm afraid to say.

It seems as if everyone has got some kind of problem. Well, first of all things, there's Mr Campbell. He's just lost his wallet and passport.
BILL: Well, I suggest he tells the police.
JEAN: Yes, I know, but I'll have to go with him as he doesn't speak a word of Spanish. Now, Mr and Mrs Seymour's room is much too noisy . . . they're in the double one over the disco. I do think we could move them somewhere away from all the noise.
BILL: Yes, the music does go on quite late.

Now listen and read aloud what Jean says.

STRUCTURE REVIEW

STRUCTURES	EXERCISES
Look back at Unit 26 and complete the boxes.	**Now play the cassette.**

STRUCTURES

Look back at Unit 26 and complete the boxes.

I suggest	he she . . .	the police.
	we . . . call they	

Perhaps I think	he she could we should you 'd better they	phone the airline. change the ticket. move to another room.
If I . . . (person), I'd		

Let's Why . . . we	have a meal (?)
What How about	. . . a meal?

I'll . . . I	call the police (?)

OK, thank you very much.
No, it's all . . . . I'll do that.

I'll	phone him. write to her. meet the plane.

EXERCISES

Now play the cassette.

26.1 Make suggestions.

Why don't we have something to eat?
I suggest we go to a restaurant.

Bill could take more exercise.
I suggest he goes running.

a) we/have something to eat/go to a restaurant
b) Bill/take more exercise/go running
c) they/take a break/have a holiday
d) we/get Mum a present/give her a book
e) you/have an early night/stay at home
f) Jean/enjoy life more/stop worrying

26.2 Offer to do things.

Offer to answer the phone.
I'll answer the phone.

Offer to type the letter.
Shall I type the letter?

Use 'I'll' and 'Shall I' in turn.

a) answer the phone   d) make some coffee
b) type the letter   e) change the light bulb
c) book the tickets   f) turn off the radio

26.3 Make promises.

Promise to be careful.
I'll be careful.

Promise not to drive too fast.
I won't drive too fast.

a) be careful   d) not lose the keys
b) not drive too fast   e) bring it back tomorrow
c) look after the car   f) not be late

Unit 27 Discussing future possibilities

🔊 PRONUNCIATION

27.1 Underline the most important words in this passage and cross out the other words.

It's four thirty in the afternoon on a tropical island in the Indian Ocean not far from the Equator. And this is the Otter Aquatic Club, a swimming club in a residential suburb of Colombo, the capital of Sri Lanka. On the verandah of a building near the pool, a thirteen-year-old Sri Lankan is playing table tennis. His opponent is a tall man of nearly seventy, dressed in shorts, sports shirt, and wearing a hearing aid. It's Arthur C. Clarke, the author of over sixty books of science fact and fiction.

Now listen and check if the words you underlined are stressed.
Then read the passage aloud.

27.2 Listen and put a ⋌ in the written version when you hear some extra words.

Clarke was born in England, but has lived in Sri Lanka since 1957. He started writing fiction at school and continued when he joined the Civil Service at the age of nineteen. Since then, many predictions he has made in his stories have become fact. In 1938 he predicted Star Wars. Seven years later he published an article explaining how satellites could be used for communication in the future. In 1951 he wrote the story *The Sentinel*, and this was the source for the film *2001: A Space Odyssey*, seventeen years later.

Listen again and write in the missing words. Choose from these words; some of them can be used more than once:

the sure mostly Somerset men of signs closely science off possibility networks short main relieved released

Now read the passage aloud.

STRUCTURE REVIEW

STRUCTURES

Look back at Unit 27 and complete the boxes.

I We They	get up have lunch	at (*time*).
He She	. . . up has lunch	

🔊 EXERCISES

Now play the cassette.

27.1 Ask about people's routine.

Jean got up at 6.30 this morning.
Does she always get up at 6.30?

a) Jean/get up/at 6.30
b) Bill/have breakfast/at 9.00
c) Annie/start work/at 9.30
d) Robert/play tennis/in the afternoon
e) Annette/watch TV/after dinner
f) the children/go to bed/8.30

If	I were rich and famous,	. . . live on a tropical island.
	I met someone from outer space,	I . . . know what to say.

27.2 Say what would or wouldn't happen.

What would Annie do if she saved enough money?
If Annie saved enough money, she'd visit Canada.

What would happen if the team trained regularly?
If the team trained regularly, they wouldn't play so badly.

a) Annie/save enough money/visit Canada
b) the team/train regularly/not play so badly
c) Jean/not so busy/paint her new flat
d) I/have to live on another planet/not be happy
e) David/have more time/take a tour round Sri Lanka

Unit 28   Making deductions

PRONUNCIATION

28.1 Underline the stressed words in this dialogue. Then mark the intonation with arrows.

WOMAN: Good morning, I'd like to confirm my flight back to Milan, please.

OFFICIAL: Yes, madam. What's your name, please?

WOMAN: Ridley – that's R–I–D–L–E–Y.

OFFICIAL: And could you tell me your flight number?

WOMAN: BA 510 leaving on Sunday morning at 9.15.

OFFICIAL: Right, your flight is confirmed. Please check in at least an hour before departure.

Now listen and check.
Then listen and read aloud what the official says.

28.2 Some of the words in the written version of the dialogue below have been changed. Listen and correct any words which are different from what you hear.

OFFICIAL: Good morning, mister. Can I see you tick it?

MAN: Yes, here you are.

OFFICIAL: Smoker or not smoker?

MAN: Non-smoking, please. A window seat if possible.

OFFICIAL: No smoking by the wing door. Do you have many hand baggage?

MAN: Just my briefcase.

OFFICIAL: Right. He's your boarding card. Have a nice fight.

Now listen and check.
Then listen and read aloud what the official says in your corrected version.

STRUCTURE REVIEW

STRUCTURES	EXERCISES
Look back at Unit 28 and complete the boxes.	**Now play the cassette.**

It looks	you're he's she's they're	buying a ticket. hungry.
	. . .	going to rain.

28.1 Make deductions about these situations.

Jean is standing outside the cinema.
It looks as if she's waiting for someone.

a) Jean/stand outside cinema/wait for someone
b) a couple/talk to the receptionist/check in
c) the sky/be very dark/be going to rain
d) Bill/sit with his eyes closed/be asleep
e) Annie/run along the street/try to catch a bus
f) the students/be very quiet/work hard

He She	looks	. . .	a doctor. an American.
They	look		students.

He She	may might could	. . .	a teacher. English.
They			policemen.

28.2 Make deductions about these people.

She might be a dancer.
Yes, she looks like a dancer.

They could be tourists.
Yes, they look like tourists.

a) she/dancer
b) they/tourists
c) he/politician
d) they/Italians
e) she/writer
f) he/spy

He She	may might could	. . .	left the country. stolen some money.

28.3 You arranged to meet a friend for dinner. Discuss what's happened to him.

Perhaps he's missed the train.
Yes, he could have missed the train.

Perhaps he's had an accident.
Yes, he might have had an accident.

a) miss train/could have
b) have an accident/might have
c) change his mind/may have
d) lost the address/could have
e) gone to another restaurant/may have
f) forget/might have

Unit 29   Expressing doubt and certainty

🔲 PRONUNCIATION

29.1 **Listen and repeat.**

I'm sure it is.

I'm sure they will.

I'm sure he didn't.

I'm sure we won't.

I'm sure it wasn't.

I'm sure she wouldn't.

Now mark the intonation with an arrow.

29.2 **Listen and mark the intonation on the question tags with an arrow.**

She wouldn't do that, would she?

That wasn't the telephone, was it?

He didn't leave his wallet on the train, did he?

It is leather, isn't it?

They'll get here soon, won't they?

We won't be late, will we?

Now read the sentences aloud.

29.3 **Listen to exercise 2 again and respond. Use the sentences in exercise 1. They are not in the right order.**

STRUCTURE REVIEW

STRUCTURES

Look back at Unit 29 and complete the boxes.

I He She It	. . .	supposed . . .	to	be at the station. arrive on time.
We You They	were			

🔲 EXERCISES

Now play the cassette.

29.1 **Say what was supposed to happen.**

The holiday was very expensive.
It was supposed to be cheap.

Robert got up late.
He was meant to get up early.

Use 'supposed to' and 'meant to' in turn.

a) the holiday was very expensive/cheap
b) Robert got up late/early
c) we went to the Royal Hotel/Grand Hotel
d) the plane arrived at 8.30/7.30
e) the students spoke in Spanish/English
f) Annie phoned her mother this morning/last night

He She They	must . . .	have	seen the film. lost the ticket.

29.2 Draw conclusions.

The film made Bill laugh.
It must have been funny.

The passengers don't know where to go.
They can't have heard the announcement.

Use 'must have' and 'can't have' in turn.

a) The film made Bill laugh/be funny
b) The passengers don't know where to go/hear the announcement
c) Robert couldn't find his ticket/be worried
d) David was very busy in Sri Lanka/have much free time
e) Annie has lost her umbrella/leave it on the bus
f) Jean was surprised to hear the news/read the papers

I'm sure	he she it	is(n't). has(n't). was(n't).
	we . . . they	did(n't). will/won't. can/can't.

29.3 Give reassurance.

The bank's still open, isn't it?
I'm sure it is.

I hope Jean didn't feel angry.
I'm sure she didn't.

a) The bank's still open, isn't it?
b) I hope Jean didn't feel angry.
c) David wasn't hurt, was he?
d) They can swim, can't they?
e) We haven't missed the plane, have we?
f) I hope I pass the exam.

I You He She We They	will . . .	have to	book tickets. go to school.

29.4 Say what people will or won't have to do.

Robert didn't reconfirm his flight today.
He'll have to reconfirm his flight tomorrow.

Jean went to the airport today.
She won't have to go to the airport tomorrow.

a) Robert didn't reconfirm his flight today.
b) Jean went to the airport today.
c) Bill can't collect the tickets today.
d) Annie did the washing today.
e) David didn't write his report today.